THE SIGN OF CHRIST

Darrell K. Jackson

The Sign of Christ
Copyright © 2022 by Darrell K. Jackson
Originally Printed in 2014

Library of Congress Control Number:	2022912429
ISBN-13: Paperback:	978-1-64749-790-3
Hardback:	978-1-64749-791-0
ePub:	978-1-64749-792-7

All rights reserved. No part of this publication may be reproduced, distributed, or transmitted in any form or by any means, including photocopying, recording, or other electronic or mechanical methods, without the prior written permission of the publisher or author, except in the case of brief quotations embodied in critical reviews and certain other noncommercial uses permitted by copyright law.

Although every precaution has been taken to verify the accuracy of the information contained herein, the author and publisher assume no responsibility for any errors or omissions. No liability is assumed for damages that may result from the use of information contained within.

Printed in the United States of America

GoTo Publish

GoToPublish LLC
1-888-337-1724
www.gotopublish.com
info@gotopublish.com

CONTENTS

Acknowledgments vii
Chapter 1 Beginnings 1
Chapter 2 The Kneeling, Praying, King and High Priest
            "Jesus" as he entered the Holy of Holies at
            the Ark of the Covenant in Heaven 9
Chapter 3 The first Scene found 27
Chapter 4 'The Throne of God & 'The Whole Duty
            of Man 39
Chapter 5 'The Cross' 59
Chapter 6 'The Good Shepherd' 69
Chapter 7 "The location of an image of HELL" 87
Chapter 8 "The Sounding of the Shofar" 97

PREFACE

As a Bible teacher, artist, and illustrator, I hope to convey a wonderful revelation of God with this book. If you are so inclined, as you read and go to Google Earth, please remember that sand is always moving around and changes are made. It will be to your great advantage if you go and view the video at my website, www.timeclockrevelation.com. You will see many of the satellite photos and comparative artwork and many that are not in this book. Some of the main pictures that have remained constant without change are the Abrahamic covenant, pictures relating to the birth of Jesus, his crucifixion, and the shepherds taking care of sheep and lambs. My discerning eye has seen an aspect of revealing facts that the very large continental land peninsula of Saudi Arabia, and the Eastern edge of Egypt as well as Turkey presents itself as a representation of Jesus our 'King of Kings' and 'High Priest'. I provide drawings that show the locations of pictures within this land area, that the mountain rock, tributaries, boulders, and sand, the things that exist topographically on the surface of that area actually form these pictures. I have also made painted illustrations that will help you identify the images to be used as comparatives to the satellite photos. Google Earth does not allow any images to be copied, so no satellite photos can be printed in this book. Every picture directly relates to bible scripture. Bible scriptures are included that directly reference specific subject matter in these pictures that God created. And with these evidences we can see fulfillment for today. Some of these scriptures did not have obvious meaning until today when we see exactly what the words say in pictures on the earth. I have detailed to the best of my ability a structured message that God is telling us through the arrangement of these pictures.

The message is this: "**Look down from on high and you will see that it is Jesus my only son, your High Priest and King of Kings by evidence of the wounds he suffered on the cross to redeem you. I Father God, created a covenant with Abraham, to establish the blood line for my son Jesus to be born into the world. God's children must appear before the judgment seat of Christ to receive according to your life that you have lived, so be careful how you live your life. My son Jesus is real. Here are his baby pictures! Here are pictures of his ministry with disciples. Here also, are pictures of his crucifixion. Set before you is life or death. You are my sheep that I love dearly. I want you to cross over into a life of protection by shepherds of whom I have chosen that must follow my Son's example of the Good Shepherd. Attention! Pray!"**

Scriptures pertaining to the image on the cover of this book will be given special meaning, literally expressed in pictorial form are presented in this book. These are Acts 2:19, Ephesians 1:10, Isaiah 40:21-22, Isaiah 40:26, Isaiah 53:1-12, Jeremiah 17:12, and Heb.9:12.

ACKNOWLEDGMENTS

I am extremely thankful that my Heavenly Father gave me this assignment, gave me the love and encouragement of his son Jesus, and the teaching and guidance of his Holy Spirit (John 14:26). I give a lot of scripture in this book because every picture that God created on the surface of the earth is literally scripture illustrated by God in pictures.

Although my wife passed away in January of 2019 I am thankful for my wife's patience during the many long hours I have spent writing this book and painting the many illustrations for you to see.

Revelation

Although revelations of later days have always fascinated me, I never imagined I would receive a revelation from the Lord in its scope. Anyone watching world news today can see that world events unfold in a way that tends to emphasize the prophecy of the latter day. While I was working on my computer late one evening, I took a break from the routine and activated a Google Earth satellite view of the Earth. When the view of the Earth satellite came up, I watched as the blue and green planet came into full view. I examined the blue oceans and the colorful green continents. How beautiful the world God created. There are so many places I want to see for myself: beautiful mountain ranges, forests, deserts, and tropical jungles with a deep dark green color. For a moment, I thought to look at the Middle East. I thought it would be interesting to look at some areas that have been in the news lately. As I zoomed in on the Arabian Peninsula, I rotated the view a little and just sat there looking at it for a moment.

Suddenly, what I saw before my eyes seemed unusual! The Scriptures of Old Testament prophecy come to mind when I see what is before me. As an artist, I can easily visualize some things. I see Jesus kneel and pray! Right there on the computer screen, the size of a continent of land! What a sight to behold. What I observe makes sense, because I remember references from the Bible that describe how Jesus was crucified, and the exact wounds that were inflicted on his body exactly as they had occurred. And right in front of me, all these wounds are visible as a day! To see this, you must rotate the Saudi Arabian Peninsula so that it is oriented the same as on the front cover of this book. Did God plan this from the beginning of creation, to show the world a picture of his living Son when the right time came? Now, a time when satellite photography is possible in full color? If anyone in any country has access to a home computer to view this type of thing today? This great image of Christ is only the beginning. Later in this book, you will see other images that show biblical events within this land mass.

I strongly encourage you to look at the Google Earth satellite map view and see for yourself, not just take my word for it in this book. Anyone with a home computer can access this information. I use a large flat screen TV, but you can also use your laptop.

The next day after my discovery, I was reluctant to believe I had discovered a biblical sign. I prayed about the phenomenon that had fascinated me, and asked for wisdom and confirmation of the scripture that came to mind to settle the idea of what I was seeing. At that time, all I had discovered was the gigantic mass picture of Jesus as a high priest and King kneeling and praying.

A few weeks later, I had the inclination to read the most important prophecies, starting with Isaiah, which was triggered by the memory of this verse in Isaiah chapter 40. The name Isaiah means "salvation of the Lord." He continued his ministry in Judah during the reign of four kings, possibly 740 to 680 years before Christ. I remembered that Isaiah wrote many things about the nations of the earth, Israel, Judah, and Messianic prophecies that predicted Christ's birth. All the verses are in Isaiah, Christ's birth foretold (7:14, 9:6), His Deity (9:6-7), His Ministry (9:1-2,42:1-7; 61:1-2), and His death (52:1-53:12). I studied Isaiah chapter 40 when I came to verses 21-22 and then verse 26, as I had already thought.

In verse 21 KJV, Isaiah seems to shout from the top of his lungs, *"Have you not known? Have ye not heard? Hath it not been told you from the beginning? Have you not understood from the foundations of the earth? It is HE who sitteth upon the circle of the earth,"* (KJV).

It seems as though Isaiah was looking at you and I in our time in a vision, and he was amazed and exasperated that this huge image of Christ is here on earth, and no one realized that is there!" When I read verse 22…"it is HE who sits on the circle of the earth" that I realized exactly who Isaiah was talking about. And when I read on, and came to verse 26"Lift up your eyes on high, and behold who hath created these things." Well, that seemed to underline the fact altogether. Only at this time in our history can we lift our eyes, so to speak, as viewing from a satellite. Yes, what I have been looking at from a satellite view is truly an image of Jesus our Christ, and I hear quite clearly Isaiah has proclaimed its wonderful revealing thousands of years ago.

What a wonderful afternoon for me. God has opened a door of understanding that has been closed for thousands of years. This mass image of the country probably existed since the time of Genesis. I could hardly wait to tell my wife. I walked into the living room and said, "Honey, do you remember the picture I showed you not long ago of what I thought seemed like Jesus kneeling and praying?" Memory serves me correctly, with the help of God. I found the reference scriptures in the book of Isaiah that seem to confirm it

After reading the scripture out loud, I looked up at her and a smile began to show on her face. We both looked at the large drawings I had set up in our living room of this picture and just stood in awe.

A short time later, I sketched a rough drawing of Jesus kneeling and praying on a sheet of paper, and showed it to a good friend of mine, who I consider a knowledgeable person when it comes to biblical things, but not an artistic sort of person. He could not visualize what I saw, so I didn't want to spring the bible verse information yet. Only disappointed, not discouraged, I decided to show it to some unsuspecting person to see what their response would be. A few days later, I had it folded in my shirt pocket while at a local bank. I showed it to a few people there, and they both were amazed. I then showed this sketch to a few more people and got the same surprised response from both persons. It was like a cute mind trick of the eye to them, and they were surprised. I took their response at face value and pursued a fuller understanding for myself.

Please keep the following thought in mind:

When you go to Google Earth looking for these images, some will not jump out at you plainly. God has not changed the fact that this large area has a considerable amount of blowing sand, and it is still moving, and God creates new images where another once was. But some are as plain to see as the nose on your face, which is constantly before us and never changes, such as the birth of Christ scenes in the land of Aseer and the scenes of the Crucifixion. I started working on this project in 2011, and God created a steady succession of newly created images by 2020 and beyond. Sometimes he blows away sand to reveal a picture, sometimes he blows sand into a configuration to create a new picture.

The Jews Seek a Sign

During the ministry of Jesus, Jewish religious leaders demanded a sign. Jesus knew they were inquiring from their carnal mind, rather than precisely deriving from the (presently existing Old Testament prophecies of the Messiah), which identified the newly arrived Messiah Jesus in detail. Matthew 12: 38-41, the certain scribes and the Pharisees answered and said, Master, we would seek a sign from you. But he answered and said to them, an evil and adulterous generation seeks a sign; and there will be no sign to it, but the sign of the prophet Jonas: For Jonas was three days and three nights in the belly of the whales; so shall the son of man be three days and three nights in the heart of the earth. The men of Nineveh repented at Jonas's preaching (turned away from sin and unbelief), and behold, a greater than Jonas is here. (See also Mt. 16:4, Mk. 11:29-30.)

God had established prophecies in the Old Testament, as recorded by Isaiah 500 to 600 years before Jesus was born. These scriptures describing the Messiah should be the guiding light of the revelation of wisdom by God to the Jews of this generation. But this generation did not repent (turn away from their sin and unbelief), as did the people of Nineveh. Therefore, the Jews of this generation failed in their own knowledge and met the judgment of God by scattering these people after the temple was destroyed in their captivity in 70 AD. *I Corinthians 1:22-25, "For the Jews require a sign, and the Greeks seek after wisdom:*

But we preach Christ crucified, unto the Jews a stumbling block, and to the Greeks foolishness; but unto them which are called, both Jews and Greeks, Christ the Power of God, and the wisdom of God. Because the foolishness of God is wiser than men; and the weakness of God is stronger than men." Again in Mark 8:11-12, *"And the Pharisees came forth, and began to question with him, seeking of him a sign from heaven, tempting him. And he sighed deeply in his spirit, and saith, why doth this generation seek after a sign? Verily, I say unto you, there shall no sign be given to this generation."*

Jesus did not want his people of this generation to focus on his power over creation. Jesus wanted his people to focus on his redemption of man, the prophecies of one coming, and now it is to provide the salvation of man. Prophecies that describe the only and only Messiah, Jesus! The chosen people of God, the Jews, had the opportunity in this generation to spread the gospel throughout the world. They did not recognize him for who he was—the Messiah! The great commission was given to the gentiles to spread the Gospel of Jesus. In Romans 14: 16, the Apostle Paul wrote that *I should be the minister of Jesus Christ to the Gentiles, ministering the Gospel of God, so that the offering of the Gentiles could be acceptable and sanctified by the Holy Spirit.* And in verse 21, *"But as it is written, to whom He [Jesus] was not spoken of, they shall see; and they who have not heard shall understand."*

Today, all people around the world can look down on the earth and see the story of redemption on the surface of the earth. And this collection of images of illustrated scripture is WITHIN THE LARGE KNEELING JESUS! Another mystery within the Word of God, which shows his power and great glory over his creation, is displayed here on earth for a sign and a series of signs for the Jews and you and me. We read in Luke 2:11, "And great earthquakes shall be in divers places, and famines, and pestilences; and fearful sights and Great Signs shall there be from heaven."

With every new discovery, I was absolutely in awe. To think that these images on Earth could have existed since the time of Genesis, and that I see them for the first time since creation! I was also surprised to learn that these are real images of real people who lived thousands of years ago. A calm but exciting and joyful emotion passed through me. I know that you will have similar experiences when you see these landscape-based images for yourself.

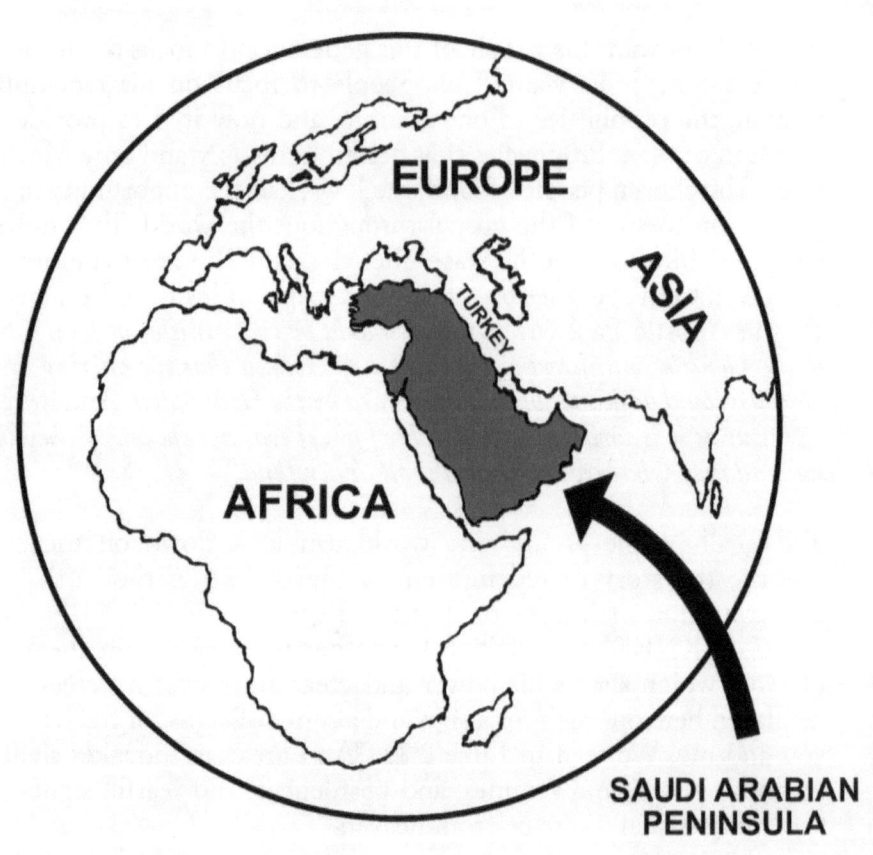

CHAPTER 1
Beginnings

As with every event, as with every step of certainty, there is a beginning. In this second printing, I have written to express the background and experiences God gave. Dreams and visions have revealed that Heavenly Father had placed in my path, as if blowing away sand from a step stone path. Yes, I am honored to be involved by God in such a mission. God has been good to me in preparing the path of my life towards the revelation and gathering of this magnificent work of God. It is the trust, faith and hope of the Heavenly Father, as he guides me to focus centrally on the achievement.

Every picture God created on the Earth's surface is Bible scripture literally expressed in picture form. All the God given, spirit led established foundational facts are set forth. The factual evidence locked in a mystery in Bible scripture. In seeing, we realize, in reading, we realize. Understanding the astronomical odds that all rocks, boulders, sand grains, etc. fall into place to form zillions of coincidences just to form one of the pictures in a collection of many is certainly not coincidental.

Purposeful renderings that make up the "moves of God" give us a direction in the path of life to achieve what He puts before us.

All this began when I looked back at the time when the Lord gave me a dream, which gave me pause to think wow, what is that all about! At the time, I worked as a drafter for a large communications company in Kansas City, producing and recording engineering data records. This dream happened 12 years before any of this began, long before I had any idea of any of this subject. In the dream, I saw a large map of Texas that was all white space, with the exception of a large geographic area in the middle of the state. This area was a prominent area. Above it were the words "Ministry Completeness." The next morning, I remembered the dream in detail. It was clear and colorful, but perplexing. If I look back years later, I can now see the relevance. Since then, my wife and I have moved back to Texas and ended up in Killeen, in the middle of Texas, without even trying to do so, as the company I worked for has moved us there.

The Formative Times

As I grew up, my mother lovingly took care of us and guided our understanding of the Bible. Yes, my mother knew when to inject Godly wisdom and understanding. She came from a culture that grew up enduring hardship, as was her father during the "Great Depression." Mother grew up without father; there was no adequate medical treatment for Brits disease in the early 1920s. And dad grew up without his mother, she died in child birth. Both mother and father saw and experienced the life changes through the Depression Era, Civilian Conservation Corp. and World War II, as dad served his five years within that global conflict. The fortitude inherent in both ingenuity and character was passed on to their sons.

Every summer, we grew a big garden with lots of different kinds of vegetables. The summer dinner table was set with plenty, and no one went hungry from their table. Mother canned fruits and vegetables from abundance to use during the winter. She was also known as a fine baker in our rural neighborhood. One of our neighbors called us the Pillsbury's.

The fruit orchard in which I played as a child yielded baskets full of peaches and plumbs, to a bountiful amount in most years. I remember laying on the grassy hill above the orchard with my head in my hands, looking out over the landscape below in the summer. I watched cars and oilfield trucks go by on the rural highway in front of our home below. I pondered the future then and wondered what and where I would be later in life.

One of my earliest favorite pastimes in childhood was to look through colorful illustrated encyclopedias and ask my mother what was written about the colorful pictures. I had childhood thoughts of saying to God; I sure would like to do beautiful pictures like that. I suppose that was the early development interest that would set me on a path toward becoming a draftsman and illustrator. No doubt, Father God heard the thoughts of that little boy.

Oh how I loved growing up in the tall pine forests of the East Texas area. When I was a small boy, I loved playing in those woods with my childhood friends, playing tag, king of the mountain, army soldiers and such. With great neighbors around us, we were allowed to hunt, fish and explore nature in almost every direction, as we were a few miles from the city. What I loved most of all was the farm chores I did for my father. Dad worked as a mechanic in a nearby small town, and we had a small farm that raised cattle, chickens and pigs, as you would normally find in any rural homestead. Those were the cherished days of boyhood. Father was inclined to support that lifestyle of our family, and I loved it. There was an occasion when my mother, father and I drove past a house on the outskirts of Henderson, Texas. The farm had quail and pheasant in net wire enclosures. The majestic stoic pheasants, with their bright red and green head and neck, which showed beautiful plumage, slowly strutted along the length of their enclosure. Their long tail feathers gave them distinction among God's aviary creation. Those cute little quail, quickly darting in groups with sudden stops, as they curiously directed their attention to our approach.

I wanted some of those birds! I called attention to them to my mother and dad as we pulled up to a stop sign. I was anxious to add some of them to my collection for FFA (Future Farmers of America) high school projects. At that time, I was active in FFA, served as chapter reporter, and wrote a weekly newspaper article for our town's newspaper. I was also involved in a wildlife habitat program. As club reporter, I wrote the weekly column pertaining to our club activities, as well as agricultural county agent supplied facts and common farm life interests. Dad purchased a few hens and roosters of both the quail and pheasants, and boy was I happy. As soon as I got home, I was gathering net wire, posts and required materials and built those pens immediately. I remember one occasion my brother Robert and I were sitting in lawn chairs in the back yard. I got up and walked over to the quail pen and removed one of the little birds that I had grown attached to. His name was Bob White, ha-ha, I called him Bob. I sat him down in the little sandy spot on the ground, and it dusted itself in a sand bath and preened its feathers as we watched with delight. At that time, I was also involved in developing our farm into a wildlife sanctuary. I've always appreciated nature, the lush woodlands and cow pasture meadows surrounding us was a perfect adventure place. I planted forage plants, a pine tree grove, and damming up a creek for a pond. Boy was that labor intensive, but rewarding.

I remember one of my childhood friends and I went to an air show at Tyler pounds field. The show included several vintage planes of various types, including military jets and helicopters, that had renowned presence and performance in our military history.

As I look back, reminiscing to a time previous from that, the year 1970, that same airfield held a much different meaning for me at that time. My brother Robert was drafted for the Vietnam War, and we were there at pounds field to see him depart for a tour of duty in Vietnam. I also saw my brother Ronnie leave from that same runway to military training at Fort Ord, California. Seeing both brothers going off into service really bothered me, and my prayers were constant on their behalf. Robert went forth to serve as a recon Sargent in the tropical jungles of South East Asia. A time in his life that proved to be a dangerous, challenging, yet adventurous endeavor that required the depth of spiritual fortitude that only a secure Christian soul could survive, with God's protection. He once said, "I did not expect to return, but the interceding prayers of our mother reached heaven on my behalf." And I would definitely agree.

I was twelve years old when this happened. Just prior to this, Robert had expressed his wish to go on another camping trip before being deployed overseas. He had many cherished memories of previous outings on Lake Murvaul. It was a great adventure in my expectations, as a twelve year old boy at that time. It would prove to build upon a lasting relationship with my brother, which would later reveal deep spiritual truths in God's word and power.

Just prior to this time in Saxon history, there were other major military conflicts in the world. One of the most significant in terms of divine destiny was the six day war of Israel in 1967. I remember many, many national evening news reports about the conflict with clarity. It was a decisive victory, showing God's protective hand, bringing Jerusalem into fulfillment of its destiny. An amazing thing happens simultaneously in history, as many young Jewish people find their identity in Jesus as "True Messiah." God's prophetic time clock ticks ever so consistently forward to our fulfillment of dispensational completion. As I grew up, Mother would bring these world situations to my attention in view of bible prophecy. Sunday School and regular church attendance built my foundational knowledge through those years.

My college interests led me to major in commercial graphics and drafting to become an illustrator, and I excelled forward in that ambition. After graduating college, I remember praying for a job. I was anxious to get life started and out on my own. The circumstances I encountered revealed that every employer was looking for someone with job experience. One of my college lecturers set up my first job. He had received a call from an employer looking for illustrators to design yellow-page ads in telephone books. What a God-given blessing that was.

The culture around us, from which we move and leave eagerly, places us in a plan of peace. During my time in public high school and college, I saw some wrong behaviors that some of my peers were involved in, and made decisions that did not reflect how these people would end up in later years. And I have seen how early bad experiences would emerge and bite as a serpent in later years. Fortunately, we have God's blessed assurance of forgiveness through faith, and what happened decades ago is forever washed away from forgiveness. The scriptures of II Timothy 2:19-22 spell this out in detail. Those who purge themselves from injustice are a vessel to honor, be sanctified, and ready for the masters to use and prepare for every good work. The only unforgivable sin is the blasphemy of the Holy Spirit, which has never been encountered in my life. Indeed, the opposite is true. With my heart centered on the love of our Heavenly Father, through the love of God's family, he has prepared my path of life with blessing, and years or decades, I should say, in preparation for the birth of this mystery.

The Dream Language

As an analogy that hopefully describes my experience, it is a journey with memorable dream encounters. How best to describe this, you might ask? Think of a trip to a new destination where you have never been. On your journey, you see interesting sights with interesting facts, and you make a mental note of them. As you move along, you get a phone call and a video message periodically. The video contains articles and situations that are fascinating. My situation was driven and directed by God-given dreams, and God spoke directly to me. God has imparted dreams to his faithful, recorded as far as the Book of Genesis.

God knows you better than you know yourself. For the Christian, the Holy Spirit within you knows every thought and emotion. Therefore, there is a plenteous supply of information within you that God can use. Information that he can recall from memory to put together a message that can inform, warn, move you toward his plan, direct you away from harm, encourage your heart's desire to serve him, etc., just to name a few. To be certain, I must also warn that evil can inject dreams typically called nightmares. Those instill fear, or try to plant bad thoughts contrary to God's word. You should immediately mentally alert yourself out of sleep and command it to "leave in Jesus Name." If you are in deep sleep and don't wake up, most likely not remember it anyway. If it is remembered, then "bring every thought captive" into forgiveness. *II Corinthians 10:5, "Casting down imaginations, and every high thing that exalteth itself against the knowledge of God, and bringing into captivity every thought to the obedience of Christ;"*

Father God is interested in your prayers, especially when it comes to the desire of your heart to fulfill His kingdom's purpose. We do not want to reject the desire of His Heart that He has placed in us. Your task is to learn the pattern of language and to be receptive to the Holy Spirit speaking to you, which reveals the true nature of the message. First and foremost, consider Scripture that may come to mind. I do not consider myself an expert on this subject, although I have years of experience. The Divinity Code by Adam F. Thompson and Adrian Beale is an excellent resource if you want to learn more. As for myself, when I had the dream, God spoke to me and explained the dream.

The Event That Changed My Life

Of all the times I wish I had a camera phone, this event I would have described would definitely have been the one. Two weeks after finding the pictures on the earth's surface, I searched Google Earth and found another picture of Jesus' "face with a crown of thorns on a mountain top." A most astounding thing happened. I printed the picture, and there, on the print, when I looked at his own face, Jesus was as he is today. I was speechless. I ran back to my computer screen and looked, but he didn't show there on the computer screen, just on the paper print, and it faded after about 8 minutes. I personally took this as a sign. Wow, Jesus did that just for me, to inspire me to develop the whole thing? Wow, yes! That's exactly what happened.

Please pay attention to this now, because it's going to be important later.

Okay, friends, let's look at the scriptural truths and collectively acknowledge what exists. We have to go back to the reason why the priests carrying the Ark of the Covenant approached the Jordan River, and the water of the Jordan River was left and right when their feet touched the water. That happened because of what was in the Ark. Inside were the stone tablets of the original 10 commandments (Jesus is the word, John 1: 14... the word became flesh and dwelt among us). Within was also Arron's rod, which budded (Jesus overcame death with life) (see Mark 16, Mathew 28, and Luke 24). Thirdly, contained inside the Ark was a bowel of mana, (Exodus 23), Jesus is the "bread of Life" (John 6:25-59). It was the symbolic JESUS crossing the Jordan River in the Ark of the Covenant into the Promised Land; that is why the waters parted!

And when the temple was built, this Ark was placed in the Holy of Holies. It was extremely powerful; no one was allowed to touch it so that he could not die immediately.

The evening that Christ died on the cross, the large curtain covering the entrance of the Holy of Holies was torn from top to bottom untouched by any man. This act of God, opening the room to the Ark of the Covenant, giving access to the Holy of Holies to anyone, anyone could touch the Ark, its power was gone, and Jesus was gone. At this time, Jesus took the Old Testament saints from paradise to Heaven.

Now, we get to the next important fact. The human high priest was once a year required to come into the Holy of Holies to sprinkle blood onto the Ark of the Covenant (the mercy seat). This was symbolically set forth by Father God symbolically, as Jesus now went to heaven to the heavenly Ark of Covenant, carrying his blood there to the Ark in heaven. *Hebrews 9:12 neither by the blood of goats and calves,* **but by His own blood He entered once into the Holy place, having obtained eternal redemption for us.** The picture on the cover of this book is Jesus as He entered the Holy of Holies in heaven. Yes, the true Ark of the Covenant in heaven is mentioned in Revelation 11:19, and the temple of God was opened in heaven, and there was seen in His temple the Ark of His Covenant;

The Ark in the earthly temple, having lost its power when Jesus was crucified and died that afternoon, God had torn open the curtain of separation, and the Jews continued their rituals with the Ark. God would not have opened the temple so that no one could enter the established holy place and accidentally touch the earthly Ark if it had been ultimately powerful. Then the prophecy of Jerimiah was fulfilled. *Jerimiah 3: 16 And it shall come to pass, when you multiply and increase in the land, in those days, saith the Lord, they shall say no more, the Ark of the Covenant of the Lord; neither shall they come to mind, nor shall they remember it, neither shall they miss it, nor shall this be done again (KJV).* With the Ark no more having power, it was for the taking by the Romans when they sacked the temple in 70AD. One possibility of their disappearance.

CHAPTER 2
The Kneeling, Praying, King and High Priest "Jesus" as he entered the Holy of Holies at the Ark of the Covenant in Heaven

As we look at the front cover of this book, the above chapter tittle is illustrated. The first part of the image of Christ plain for me to see was the bleeding hands at the Nile River delta and the wrist where the Suez Canal was cut and I can even see the sleeve of the arm. The Nile River seems to be the blood flowing down from the hand, and the Red Sea flows down from the wrist. I then followed the arm right up toward Lebanon then Turkey. I can see a head, but…not quite… it is though the hair is draped down covering the side view of the face I then looked over the whole image area of the continent all the way down to the Arabian Sea. I now can see the bended knee and bent foot in a sandal. The sandal heel is sticking outward just as it would if the toes were bent kneeling that way. You can even see the ripples in the garment lying on the floor beside him. Amazing!

What I see now over all is Jesus kneeling and praying, having his hands out in front of him, his hands and wrist bleeding down the Nile River and the Red Sea. But what about that head area? This takes more research as you will see in later chapters. At the top of the head, the head is tilted over, bowing down, there is a linen Mitre on top of his head and a crown of gold over the top of it. Let's look at what the word of God has to say about this now.

Proverbs 25:2 it is the Glory of God to conceal a thing, KJV.

God has specific reasons to have something hidden until it is time to reveal. Remember God told Daniel to close up the book and not to reveal anything else. Time has specific purpose in God's plan.

This representation of Jesus has been in existence for thousands of years, likely from the time of Peleg when the Earth was divided (Genesis 10:25). For such a time as this, after two years of land surface research (presently years 2012 – 2013, and still ongoing). I would like to invite you on an investigative journey into this giant colossal land mass picture in its magnificent proof. As you will see later there are some very interesting smaller images deep down in various places. These dramatic images are all made by mountain ridges, deep valleys, rock formations and shades and shadows of the angle of the sun as well as different soil and sand colors. In essence it is "Art by God himself". Artistic pictures comprised of land with true meaning. I absolutely encourage you to look at it on your computer for yourself. Given the fact that these are "God Created" this has to be the discovery of the current millennium.

First of all I will quickly detail the various accurate marks that give evidence that this is an image of Christ Jesus kneeling and praying as a living person after crucifixion. More of each of these details will be further examined in later chapters.

First of all, please, look at the head area in the country of Turkey. Jesus wears a mitre. Up on the top of the head of the Hebrew High Priest there was to be a linen bonnet called a Mitre (Mitsnehfeth, a Tiara, i.e., official head adornment of a King or High Priest, a Diadem) made of linen, which represents Righteousness. On the front of this bonnet was to be a crown or plate of gold tied to the bonnet by blue ribbon or lace. The words: "Holy unto the Lord" were to be engraved upon the gold plate. Here in the Mitre and "crown of gold" is pictured the humanity and divinity of Messiah Jesus as our Priest-King!

For further understanding see diagram page titled "wound locations".

Secondly in the image you will see right below the mitre (crown) in the area of hair, there are several green mountain slope areas and lakes that are arranged in locations that represent where thorn spikes from the crown of thorns pierced the head and bled out into the hair. Third you will see in the chin area a very dark colored area representing where hairs from the beard were plucked out, and the blood drips from the chin onto the shoulder running down the Euphrates river.

Fourth you will see in the Nile River Delta the bleeding hand, and the wrist flowing down the Red Sea from the Sues Canal. Fifth you will see the lash marks on his back made by the cat of nine tails bleeding through the garment that he wears. Sixth you will see the spear wound on the chest area where blood and water flowed out. The Seventh indicator on this image is the nail scar on the foot that is bent while kneeling, it is a land scar where a land slide produced this large noticeable mark.

Of particular note we can see a salt flat in the area of Tuz Golu Turkey.

This location is the area of where the ear would be located. Jesus wants us

To know that he is listening to our prayers! Jesus said in *Mathew 5:13 ye are the salt of the earth: but if the salt (the Christian) have lost his savour (strength, quality) wherewith shall it be salted? It is thenceforth good for nothing, but to be cast out, and to be trodden under foot of man. KJV*

Footnote: From "Pictures of Messiah" by Ruth Specter Lascelle

Let's remember the following to be sure that we are following biblically in line with the Word of God concerning this image we see.

Exodus 20:4 Thou shalt not make unto thee any graven image, or any likeness of any thing that is in Heaven above, or that is in the Earth beneath, or that is in the water under the Earth (KJV).

Let's agree that this is not a graven image made by man. This large land mass is 2,311 miles across from head to knee and over 1,217 miles wide. We are not to worship an image of the creator, only the Creator himself. Is there any reason that the hair is draped down covering the face? There is no way man could have created this. In fact, at the moment I'm writing this…I'm the only man I know that realizes that it exists.

Deuteronomy 29:29 The secret things belong unto the Lord our God: but those things which are revealed belong unto us and to our children for ever, that we may do all the words of the law (teaching) (KJV).

Notice that the prevailing winds of the Arabian Desert have not changed their flowing course over thousands of years. The sand dunes detail an image of the body in this large picture. For such a Sign to be given to man kind today it is truly magnificent.

Acts 2:19 "And I will show Signs and Wonders in Heaven above, and Signs in the Earth Beneath;(KJV)

Ephesians 1:10…of the fullness of times he might gather together in one all things in Christ, both which are in Heaven, and which are on Earth; even him.;KJV

Isaiah 33:17 "Thine eyes shall see the King in his beauty; they shall behold the land that is very far off". I know that this verse has been millennial in view point, and could it also be present tense as well for today we can see our King of Kings in a land far off by which was created by our all mighty Creator?

By these scripture references as well as others in later chapters, you can see a foretelling of this for today. In Ephesians 1:10 …gather together all things in Christ of course means his ultimate sacrifice has made the total all encompassing payment for our sins past and future for you and I. And since all things are all things can it also pertain to this sign on Earth: even him;

Revelation 14:7 …Worship him that made heaven, and earth, and the sea, and the fountains of waters,(KJV).

Revelation 1:5 …The Prince of the Kings of the earth for the Lord is a Great God, and a Great King above all Gods (KJV).

In Revelation 19:13 it states "And he (Jesus) was clothed with a vesture dipped in blood: and his name is called the "Word of God". This Sign and Wonder clearly shows the blood upon the garment (vesture) that he wears.

In first John 5:8 it says *"And there are three that bear witness in earth, the Spirit, and the water, and the blood: and these three agree in one. If we receive the witness of men, the witness of God is Greater: for this is the witness of God which he hath testified of his Son. He that believeth on the Son hath the witness in himself: he that believeth not God hath made him a liar; because he believeth not the record that God gave of his Son. And this is the record, that God hath given to us eternal life, and this life is in his Son.(KJV)*

As mentioned above "the witness of God is Greater" please keep this thought in mind as you read on and find out all of the many SIGN's in picture form that God has created.

Another dream

One summer night after writing down some research data, of pictures and bible scripture I quit work, had a time of prayer, then got ready for bed. I had drifted off into a peaceful sleep more settled than typical of my routine sleep times. At a time that was past mid-night in the early morning hours I had a vivid dream. It was brief but very real and colorful; I emphasize the word colorful due to the fact that the item displayed to me in the dream held special meaning in its color. In the dream I was sitting in a chair, and two hands came toward me holding a red neck tie and laid it gently across my lap. It was the brightest red, no other color, totally red. I remember hearing "This will be my signature upon you." The next morning, I pondered the significance of the dream. I then thought "without Jesus' shedding of blood, there is no remission of sin." Could that be the significance of the red color? I decided, Yes! That must be it.

The Crown of Thorns

Why a crown of thorns? In *Mathew 27:29 And when the (roman soldiers) had platted a crown of thorns, they put it upon his head, and a reed in his right hand: and they bowed the knee before him, and mocked him saying, hail, King of the Jews!(KJV)*

Let us now compare this mock crown to a true crown. A true crown of a King is typically made of gold, the most rare and valuable of all metals of the highest quality signifying divine headship, an adornment of the head. Why adorn the head? This draws attention to the one part of the body that is responsible for decision making, planning, administering and ruling. Why a crown of Thorns? If you read Genesis 3 verse 17 starting in the second half of verse 17 …cursed is the ground for thy (mans) sake; in sorrow shalt thou eat of it all the days of thy life; Thorns also thistles shall it bring forth to thee; KJV.

A crown of thorns was used by the soldiers out of a disobedient sinful mindset (and I think unaware of its significance). The crown of thorns is a symbol of mans fall from Grace, mans original sin, life and death curse of which Christ was paying for on the cross. The Roman soldiers did not know this; they were just following their natural sin nature.

Why were hairs of the beard of Jesus ripped out? Why was his body cut? In Leviticus 21:1&5 we see the directions given from God to Moses concerning the Priests …speak unto the priests the sons of Aaron, and say unto them, there shall none be defiled for the dead among his people. *Verse 5 They shall not make baldness upon their head, neither shall they shave off the corner of their beard, nor make any cuttings in their flesh.(KJV)*

So, we see evil sinful works of ripping hair from Jesus beard by their evil imagination yet also attacking his High Priest & King position at the same time. Jesus' back was cut several times by the cat of nine tails. We can not be sure that the roman soldiers respected the Jewish rule of only 39 stripes… they could have done much more. And his hands and feet were pierced by nails onto the wooden cross. The very last wound that Jesus' body took was the piercing of his body with the Roman spear to make sure he was dead. Water and blood gushed forth from the wound. Each time one of these wounds was inflicted to his body he was delivering us from the curse of sin and death. Jesus paid the ultimate price for us conquering sin and death for all of us. Jesus is the First begotten of the dead Revelation 1:5 He lives and we will live after death also if we have placed our faith in Jesus.

I Corinthians 2:7-8 But we speak the wisdom of God in a mystery, even the hidden wisdom, which God ordained before the world unto our glory: Which none of the princes (evil fallen angels) of this world knew: for had they known it, they would not have crucified the Lord of Glory, (KJV).

The Very Significance of each wound

1. Crown of thorns from evil demonic attack on his position of High Priest and King of Kings, (Psalms 8:5, 21:3, 103:4, 132:18, Isaiah 28:5, 62:3).

2. Ripping out hair from his beard attacked his Levitical Priesthood, (Lev.21:5, Isaiah 53:1-12).

3. The hands were wounded by evil intent attacking his Righteousness (II Corinthians 6:7, Gen. 49:24).

4. His feet were evilly attacked being nailed to the cross, attacking the symbol of his spreading the gospel of truth. Also to attack his total dominion, all things are under his feet! (Psalm 8:6, 22:26, Isaiah 52:7).

5. His back was slashed, torn, cut, attacking his Levitical Priesthood (Leviticus 21:5, Isaiah 53:5)

6. Lastly His Heart was pierced, the evil ones influenced men to pierce his heart with a spear to attack the loving compassion (Psalm 22:14, 33:11, 37:31, 40:10, Isaiah 51:7, 63:4, Jeremiah 3:15).

The number six is the number of man, with the final wound that signified final physical death; it also established final victory for mankind. The absolute most that God could do to save mankind was to come down among us as a compassionate loving man and allow evil to do what it thought would be an evil victory which was a terrible failure. Jesus showed life after death as an example for you and me. All we have to do is accept this very fact (Romans 10:8-13). By doing so you then at that moment become a Christian, (SAVED). Saved from an evil eternity, hell. Saved as in given access to the knowledge of God's loving compassionate will. Saved, as in gaining access to God's perfect wisdom, to establish a blessed, stabilized life. Saved, as in gaining access to God's healing, for the physical body. Saved, as in gaining access to the healing of spiritual issues. Saved, as in gaining access to learning how to be a blessing to others.

More clues to the SIGN

1. In Isaiah 40:21 "Have ye not known? Have you not heard? Hath it not been told you from the beginning? Have ye not understood from the foundations of the earth? It is HE (Jesus) that sitteth upon the circle of the earth...This scripture applies to the picture on the front of the book.

Isaiah 40:26 Lift up your eyes ON HIGH, and behold who hath created these things, ...that bringeth out their host by number: (every tribe was numbered) he calleth them all by names by the Greatness of His Might, for He is Strong in Power; not one faileth, (KJV).

Why would God tell us to look down on the earth from up on high unless there was something to see? Today with satellite visual capability we indeed can lift our eyes on high and look and see who it is on the circle of the earth who created these things.

Yes Jesus has existed from eternity past (a theophany). Before the earth was created, he was present when the earth was created. Please read *Proverbs 8; 22 The Lord possessed me in the beginning of his way, before his works of old. I (Jesus) was set up from everlasting, from the beginning, or ever the earth was. When there were no depths, I (Jesus) was brought forth; when there were no fountains abounding with water, before mountains were settled, before the hills was I brought forth: While as yet he had not made the earth, nor fields, nor the highest part of the dust of the world. When he prepared the heavens, I was there: when he set a compass upon the face of the depth: when he established the clouds above: when he strengthened the fountains of the deep: when he gave to the sea his decree, that the waters should not pass his commandment: when he appointed the foundations of the earth: then I was by him, as one brought up with him: and I (Jesus) was daily his delight, rejoicing always before him: rejoicing in the habitable part of the earth; and my delights were with the sons of men. Now therefore harken unto me, o ye children: for blessed are they that keep my ways.*

John 10:30 God the father and Jesus are one, (KJV).

(also see Isaiah 40:22). *Jesus said in John 5:19-20 the Son can do nothing of himself but what he seeth the father do: for what things soever he doeth, these also doeth the Son likewise, (KJV).*

And here again we see scriptural factual written Word of God telling us who this is that is pictured kneeling and praying and bleeding, crowned King of Kings and our High Priest.

Why is the face hidden from view?

As we can see on this gigantic land image the hair is draped down covering the side of the face. Let's see what the bible says about this. God of course does not want us to worship an image as stated earlier. God wants us to worship him, not an image of him. *In Isaiah 52:14 As many as were astonished at thee; his visage was so marred more than any man, and his form more than the sons of men (KJV)*

Christ was bruised, cut and bleeding. By reason that hair is draped down covering the face we also can read the following scriptures.

Isaiah 64:7 and there was none that calleth on thy name that stireth up himself to take hold of thee: for thou hast hid thy face from us. And hast consumed us (our sin), because of our iniquities. Mathew 26:67 Then did they spit in his face, and buffeted him; and others smote him with the palms of their hands, (KJV). Luke 22:64 and when they had blindfolded him, they struck him on the face, (KJV). Could it be that if he had shown the side view of his face that it would have been too obvious and too early for people to see? Later in this book you will see a location where he has made a partial front view of Christ's' face with crown of thorns for us to see. You will see this in a later chapter showing you where to look. There are areas on this land mass that have very detailed pictures of bible events showing specific people in many places.

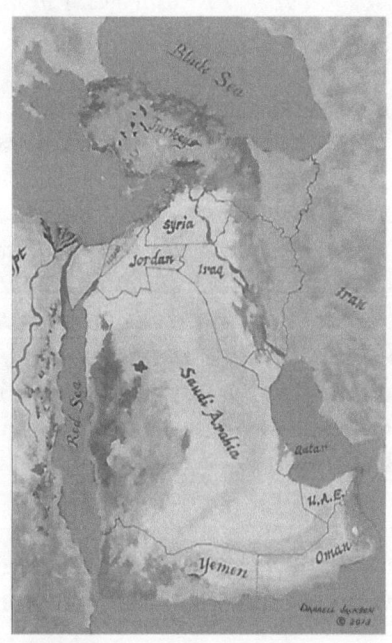

Saudi Arabian Peninsula

Jesus Kneeling and Praying,

THE SIGN OF CHRIST

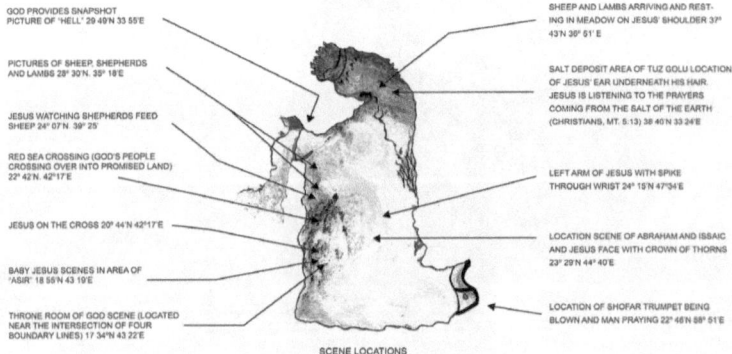

SCENE LOCATIONS

"Scene Locations"

The Spear Pierced His Side

John 19:33-34 But when they came to Jesus, and saw that he was dead already, they broke not his legs: but one of the soldiers, with a spear pierced his side, and forthwith came there out blood and water. This was prophesied before in Psalms 34:20 that "a bone of him shall not be broken and Zech. 12:10 "They shall look upon him whom they pierced."KJV

Since early scripture spoke of these things long before Christ was crucified we know that blood and water had to come forth from Christ. Yes, that was the last wound to Christ's body right after death. Let's look at the significance of this.

I John 5:8-12 "And there are three that bear witness in earth, the spirit, and water, and the blood: and these three agree in one. If we receive the witness of men, then the witness of God is Greater: for this is the witness of God which he hath testified of his Son, (KJV).

The very fact that the last wound after death was the flowing forth of blood and water is prophetic and symbolic. Let's examine this further.

Before the blood and water came forth it was the spirit that came forth. This is also prophetic and symbolic. John 19:30 he (Jesus) said it is finished: and he bowed his head, and gave up the ghost (spirit). The Spirit came forth, then the blood, then the water. Jesus said in *John 14:26 But the comforter, which is the Holy Spirit, whom the Father will send in my name, he shall teach you all things, and bring all things to your remembrance, whatsoever I have said to you, (KJV)*. Ok, next the blood. *Acts 20:28 Take heed therefore unto yourselves, and to all the flock, over the which the Holy Ghost hath made you overseers, feed the Church of God, which he hath purchased with his blood, (KJV)*. Ok, now... water. *John 4:14 But whosoever drinketh of the water that I shall give him shall never thirst: but the water that I shall give him shall be in him a well of water springing up into everlasting life, (KJV)*. Please remember symbolism is very important to God in his relationship to us, a part of his communication with us.

What does it mean for us now to have before us a pictorial representation of biblical fact? As we see fact filled pictures from high above, we can realize a designer. If there is a designer...that means there is a purpose. Can you think of anything that was ever designed that had no planned purpose? God has required our faith most of all without seeing anything tangible in order to get true faith believers. When thinking about pictures in general please consider this, God tells every believer to show a picture to everyone around them after they have become a Christian to display the death and resurrection by baptism. Jesus said: *Mathew 28:19 Go ye, therefore, and teach all nations, baptizing them in the name of the Father, and of the Son, and of the Holy Spirit…(KJV)* The act of public baptism shows that we believe in the resurrection of our body *I Thessalonians 4:16…and the dead in Christ shall rise first, (KJV).* In a separate example, something visible was done when Jesus kneeled down and wrote or drew something on the ground in John 8:8 when the woman was accused of adultery and all those gathered to stone her looked on and listened to Jesus and looked at what he had created on the ground, and they all dropped their stones and walked away.

Also consider this about visible evidence, all early hand written alphabet letters represented something pictorially such as the Ancient Hebrew letter "hey". The ancient letter 'Hey' at its beginning was a stick figure of a person with its arms out stretched as if to say "hey look at this" or "hey very important, attention, etc. This is just one example among many.

In Romans the first chapter it says that by the very creation that we see that man is without excuse. By looking at all we see around us there is the very evidence of a magnificent designer creator. So, pictures in one form or another are also a part of communication from God to us. After the flood, bringing down much of the atmospheric moisture during the great flood, God formed the 'rainbow' as a pictorial sign. There have been many pictorial signs by God over time. Man has not created these that we are looking at now, no way possible due to immense size and complicated proportion. Impossible to say these are zillions of coincidences with all the mountains and mountain valleys, rocks, boulders and grains of sand in the correct place forming all the pictures!

The Bleeding Hands and Wrist

Why do you suppose that people have a natural inclination to clasp their hands together sometimes when praying? Is it because we've seen others do it? We are not told that this must be done. Yet some people do this. Could it be that this act has some important significance in history? It would seem that by having our hands clasped together this signifies self control and signifying our humility, to be only occupied with thought and not physical activity. It is important to note that the nail driven in this area (Suez Canal)…God did not create…but man made this cut into this area. It the earliest historical records we know that men dredged out some of the soil to allow small boats to float through. As time progressed they made it larger until which time they created the larger cut called the Suez Canal. It has become a major shipping lane and is one the most valuable maritime thoroughfares in the world. In the lower half of the Saudi Arabian Desert in the area of Riyadh and southward you will see a large human left arm. And at the wrist and hand you will see a large spike going through it.

On closer inspection you will see that this entire nail or spike is covered with hundreds of green little farm sites. It is interesting that this specific site all along the length of the spike is very rich in good water for their farming purposes. Notice that the large hand has its fingers drawn back just exactly as it would if the nerves and ligaments were damaged when a spike is driven into the flesh there.

Could there be a clue in *Isaiah 53:1 "Who hath believed our report? And to whom is the arm of the Lord revealed?{KJV}* Please see video at www.timeclockrevelation.com in upper right corne of web site, or timeclockrevelation you tube.

From medical science we know that a nail through the palm of the hand would not hold up the body weight. Only a nail through the wrist would hold securely to support the weight of the body to the cross. The pictures on the surface of the earth indicate this also.

The Wound through both feet.

At the lower right where you see the foot bent while kneeling, you will see the spike scar that was made on top of the foot. The metal spike driven into the foot has left a scar for us to see. This huge mountain side has a mineral deposit of a lighter color than the surrounding soil and shows prominently there. Both feet were set together, one on top of the other and the spike driven through both. In total there are 6 wounds to the body of Christ. And since we know that 6 is the number of man we can see the association here with man's sin paid for in the blood of Christ. In total there are seven identifying markers showing the identity of Jesus Christ. First the crown of the head, crown of thorns wounds, chin wound, wounded hands, wounded back, wounded lower chest, wounded feet.

Written by men?

One of the all time favorite rebuttals of many is to say "but the bible was written by men". Actually the very first words recorded (written) were written by God on stone tablets on Mt. Sinai, the 10 Commandments. There is also the name of God written in the mountain ridge tops near Jerusalem written in Hebrew letters 'YAWEY' spelled in letters yod, hey, vov, hey.

Today with your examination of what is revealed in this book you will see visual evidence pictorially that God has recorded on earth for you to see. Please pull up a Google Earth view of this on your computer to see for yourself what is drawn by God on the land. It is virtual artwork done by God himself using the land, rock, rock formations, different colors of various minerals, sand, etc.

You will see for yourself, the manger birth scenes of Jesus, baby Jesus with Mary and Joseph, Jesus wearing crown of thorns, Abraham, Isaac, David, Moses and the Red Sea Crossing, a scene of the pit of hell that includes people, demons, skulls etc. on fire. All of these are extremely huge, made of mountain ridges, rock formations, sand, etc. formed in such a way as to realistically depict actual people and events in biblical history. There are no cartoonish looking images at all. You will see a scene of Abraham and Isaac standing with heads bowed thanking God for the sacrifice provided, you will see the ram lying there in detail, you will also see the head of a lamb floating in mid air in front of them, you will also see below the ram a visual of Jesus face with crown of thorns. All of this is visible from satellite view. All of these are miles across in size and some hundreds of miles.

Please turn to the page entitled 'Scene Locations' in order to know where these are located so you can zoom in and see each of these. I absolutely encourage you to see these from satellite view and not just take my word for it in this book.

For those of us who are trained in the word of God we can understand that men were spiritually moved by God to write down what was revealed to them. This has also become apparent with the revealing of the bible code in recent years. The bible code of Hebrew letter sequencing is so precise and mathematically proven to be of impossible odds in accidentally happening. This subject has been written about and is much too lengthy to include in this book, but is available in most Christian book stores for you to investigate if you wish to do so. As more proof is released in these recent years we can see that God truly wants us to realize his absolute reality through prophetic revelation.

A careful examination of the names and numbers in the bibles text reveals special mathematical designs and codes that are so complex that no human could have produced these significant occurrences.

Biblical information has influenced the lives of individuals, the cultures, and history of the western world in a magnificent way. Many of our major hospitals, colleges and universities were started by Christians. Love and compassion have been at the core beginnings of these institutions.

"Man can only re-create, Man can- not create."

At this point in time of my research and discovery, I've taken a break and gone to a local coffee shop. Sitting across from me is a young man reading a science article magazine and I began a conversation with him. He said he was reading an interesting article of how the medical sciences had created a new sheep from a single cell of tissue. "Really, I said?" He said I suppose, in the future they will be able to create most anything."

I said, really, create? That's a very strong word they use isn't it, create? I began saying, you know, I studied their clams recently also, and some glaring facts seem to occur. He seemed to be interested so I continued. Imagine anything new and you will see that you've only taken parts of things already in existence to make what you've imagined in your mind. It is impossible for man to think up something new or create a new base element. Gold for instance is a base element. There is no combination of elements that make up gold. Gold is the base element gold. The periodic table we all learned about in high school lists all the base elements. "Yes, I see what you mean. Excellent observation he says."

While we are on this subject for you the reader, let's take it further before going to the next chapter. How would you imagine to create an atom or molecule for instance? And to examine how really complex this is, think of the following. Let's say you wanted to create a living plant. First of all you would have to create a seed. And inside that seed you would have to create the ability within itself to remember, such as DNA (Deoxyribonucleic Acid) the cell memory, and self- replication of all living things. This would tell what type of plant to generate how to do cell division/replication, etc. It would also have to know how to recognize soil temperature, soil moisture, light or darkness, up and down direction- which direction to send forth roots, what direction is upward to send up foliage.

Modern scientist today, are seeing that DNA is so immensely complex that it could have only been designed. Scientist has only been able to re-arrange DNA strand sections. Please consider the complexity of cells in our human body for instance. Each of us, have approximately 3 trillion cells and each cell has 60,000 proteins in 100 different configurations. And science today can- not create DNA from scratch. It would be astronomically absurd to think such complexity happened by chance, and especially happened by chance for each and every creature and plant that exists. Yes, there definitely is a designer.

And on this note, for every rock, boulder, grain of sand, as well as mountain side, valley, and tributary to be accurately placed to form these many pictures, it would be equally absurd to think these were zillions of coincidences. God is getting our attention!

An important meeting

Once I had sufficient data gathered I made a trip to Glen Rose Texas to meet with Dr. Carl Baugh at the creation evidence museum. I had a collection of video as well as paper prints generated from google earth satellite photos. He carefully examined each picture and concluded that he saw everything that I pointed out, and concluded by saying that these were possibly created at the time of creation. Each, being the result of collections of rock, boulders, mountains, and mountain valleys, further positive proof. This was a good day of further confirmation.

CHAPTER 3
The first Scene found

First of all make sure you have the whole Arabian Peninsula oriented vertical just as if you are looking at Jesus kneeling and praying just like I have illustrated on the front cover of this book. If you do this then all the smaller scenes will be in correct orientation for you to see. The first picture carved in rock we see is a large left arm in the desert with a spike going through the wrist. This is located near Ryad Saudi Arabia, coordinates 24degrees 14'08.33"N and 47deg 33'28.34"E best seen at elevation 2022', eye altitude 356 miles. *Isaiah 53:1 Who hath believed our report? And to whom is the arm of the Lord revealed? (KJV)* See the large spike going through the wrist? See the fingers drawn back just exactly the way they would react when the spike driven through the nerves and ligaments of the wrist are damaged by the spike? *Isaiah 52:10 The Lord hath made bare his holy arm (the sand is blown away from it, now uncovered) in the eyes of all the nations: and all the ends of the earth shall see the salvation of our God, (KJV).* Look closely at the spike and you will see all along the length of it tiny little green irrigated farm sites watered by wells that are very productive in the area of this large spike.

In *John 4:14 But whosoever drinketh of the water that I shall give him shall never thirst: but the water that I shall give him shall be in him a well of water springing up into everlasting life, (KJV)* Ok, now notice that this is specifically a left arm. Since we know that Hebrew is written right to left we know to look left of this large arm and wow! What do we see? A scene of Abraham and Isaac on a mountain top with a ram laying beside them against a large bolder. You will find this in

THE SIGN OF CHRIST

the Al Beadhtin Mountains, coordinates 23 degrees 29'53.72"N 44 degrees 40'07.75E Elevation 3130 Feet, Eye Altitude 152.57 miles. Throughout this book you will see pictures that I have painted to help you see the same thing in Google Earth. All Google Earth satellite pictures are protected by copyright and therefore I can not simply use copies of the actual scenes in a book. I have done my best to depict each as closely to what is seen on the surface of the earth as possible with my art renderings, as you will see in the video timeclockrevelation you tube. Or you can see it in the web site www.timeclockrevelation.com where you will also find TV and radio interviews at the top of the page under "media" tab.

Abraham and Issac with their heads bowed in prayer at Sacrifice Alter with Ram, Face of Jesus with Crown of Thorns

We see now, in this moment in time have the prophetic words of Isaiah 51:1-2 fulfilled as well as Isaiah 52:10. Isaiah 51:1-2 Hearken to me, ye that follow after righteousness, ye that seek the LORD, look unto the rock whence you are hewn, and to the hole of the pit whence ye are digged. Look unto Abraham your father, and unto Sarah that bare you: for I called him alone, and blessed him, and increased him, KJV.

In Genesis 22 we read the account. God tested Abraham. God said to Abraham "Take thy son, thy only son whom thou lovest, and get thee into the land of Moriah, and offer him there for a burnt offering upon one of the mountains I will tell thee of." And Abraham rose up early in the morning, and saddled his ass and took two of his young men with him, and Isaac his son, and clave the wood for the burnt offering, and rose up, and went unto the place of which God had told him.

Then on the third day Abraham lifted up his eyes, and saw the place afar off. And Abraham said to his young men, abide ye here with the ass and I and the lad will go yonder and worship, and come again to you, and Abraham took the wood of the burnt offering, and laid it upon Isaac his son; and he took the fire in his hand, and a knife; and they went both of them together And Isaac spoke unto Abraham his father, and said, My father : and he said, Here am I, my son. And he said, Behold the fire and the wood: but where is the lamb for a burnt offering? And Abraham said My son, God will provide himself a lamb for a burnt offering: so they went both of them together. And they came to the place which God had told him of; and Abraham built an alter there, and laid the wood in order, and bound Isaac his son, and laid him on the alter upon the wood. And Abraham stretched forth his hand, and took the knife to slay his son and the angel of the lord called unto him out of heaven, and said, Abraham, Abraham and he said here am I. And he said, lay not thy hand upon the lad, neither do thou any thing unto him; for now I know that thou fearest God, seeing thou hast not withheld thy son, thine only son from me. And Abraham lifted up his eyes, and looked, and behold a ram caught in a thicket by his horns: and Abraham went and took the ram; and offered him up for a burnt offering in the stead of his son. And Abraham called the name of that place Jehovahjireh; as it is said to this day, in the mount of the Lord it shall be seen. And the angel of the Lord called unto Abraham out of heaven the second time. And said, by myself have I sworn saith the Lord, for because thou hast done this thing, and hast not withheld thy son, thine only son:

That in blessing I will bless thee, and in multiplying I will multiply thy seed as the stars of the heaven, and as the sand which is upon the sea shore, and thy seed shall possess the gate of his enemies; and in thy seed shall all the nations of the earth be blessed; because thou hast obeyed my voice, (KJV). Now examine this scene in the mountain top from further away. Now while you are viewing this scene please look at the ram. You will see Jesus face that is partly… a part of the ram's front right leg. See the crown of thorns?!!

Coordinates 23degrees 29'14.78"N 44Degrees 40'26.64"E. It is in the linage of Abraham that Jesus was born through his mother Mary. It is through Jesus that all the nations are blessed.

A very important fact filled implementation of God's will for Sarah is revealed for our learning. God showed his power and mercy for a 90 year old woman Sarah, Abraham's wife to conceive and give birth to Isaac who's descendants will become the great nation Israel. Also of great importance, the two comparison conditions, free woman Sarah Abraham's wife and bond woman Hagar a servant. God loves both and blesses the descendants of both women in the end. However, we must see the Spiritual Freedom path and the Bondage path. Sarah, a type of grace, and the "Jerusalem which is above", Galatians 4:22-31. When Sarah became wroth about the fact that she had not been able to conceive, she made a hasty wrathful decision to have Hagar provide the conception of her husband's seed. This was not God's plan. Sarah's terrible decision went entirely against God's plan of promise for the birth of their future heir. We today can get into trouble like by trying to help God in the wrong way. Father God has planned to show a miracle birth between two very old people, advanced in years, Sarah being 90 years old and Abraham 100 years of age when Isaac is born. (a miracle birth, that of Issac).

The beginning of a great nation Israel is this miracle birth of Isaac, Genesis 17:4-10. This blood line will establish a long line of descendants that will eventually lead to the birth of Jesus. Isaac is exemplified in a fourfold way (1) of the church as composed of the spiritual children of Abraham, Galatians 4:28; (2) of Christ as the son "obedient unto death" , Genesis22:1-10, Philippians 2:5-8; (3) of Christ as the bridegroom of a called-out bride, Gen.24, Mathew 16:18; (4) of the new nature of the believer as "born after the spirit", Gal. 4:29, also 21:4.

THE SIGN OF CHRIST

"Face of Jesus wearing crown of Thorns" 23 degrees
27 minutes North, 44 degrees 38 minutes East

The Blood Covenant

After these revelations thus far we must cover the blood covenant. Blood covenant rites have been known to have existed among peoples in various cultures throughout the world. In anthropological research covering the many cultures around the globe there have been evidences of satanic human sacrifices, many stone edifices used for that purpose are still visible today. God, in his infinite mercy and love put a plan in place for the end of such practices and provide a way of forgiveness for the sin of man, by placing the third part of his trinity 'Jesus' in our place. Because God wants to save man-kind from self- destruction, he came down from heaven himself to show his power over death and to provide you and I access to everlasting life. You and I have this access through placing our faith in this act of ultimate mercy.

Our Lord God performed the first animal sacrifice to cover the nakedness of Adam and Eve with animal skins, Gen. 3:8-24. In Genesis 4:3-11 we see the very first example of an animal sacrifice. Our Lord God would not accept any other sacrifice such as Cain's offering from the fruit of the ground. Only an animal sacrifice would be acceptable to God. This was to be a continuing practice among man-kind to establish a covenant that ultimately would point to the final sacrifice of Jesus on the cross. The only acceptable animals would be perfect without blemish, no disease, no health problem whatsoever. If it were a red heifer, it must not have ever been used to pull a burden with a yoke. This was to symbolize the perfect character of Jesus, the Son of God, our perfect example of a life without sin, without burden, without disease. Typically a lamb was used for sacrifice which symbolized the gentle, innocent sinless character of God. The repetition of this act over several generations was to teach man-kind this very fact. Life is in the blood, Leviticus17:11-14.

Salvation would be free by grace and mercy only. Please notice that the scene in the mountain top shows Jesus' face as part of the ram's front leg (Jesus was the substitute sacrifice). This huge land picture should further emphasize to us that Jesus is our Savior and God wants you and I in covenant with him by accepting his son Jesus.

If you would like to become a Christian please pray in your own words, "Heavenly Father, I accept your son Jesus, I know that he died and rose from the grave and lives today, and wants me in covenant with you.

Please forgive me of my sins, please come into my heart; I want to live my life for you Heavenly Father."

If you have prayed this and meant it from your heart, you are now a Christian and will have eternal life in Heaven. Please join a local New Testament church that teaches the whole Bible and tell the Pastor of that Church about this. You can then be baptized.

The Arabian Desert

In order to have some understanding of this land area we will briefly look at a historical account of exploration and some information about the topography that God used to build these amazing messages to us.

British civil servant Bertram Thomas an Englishman who went to Arabia during World War I wrote the following about his exploration of this immense desert area called the Rub'al Khali "The Empty Quarter". It was here that British servant Bertram Thomas turned his face to the desert sun. Thomas was one of the many English men who went to Arabia during World War I, when the region was at contest between Great Britain and Turkey. Unlike most, Thomas remained after the war, serving as vizier, or counselor, to the Sultan of Oman.

He left for Rub'al Khali in December 1930 on his own exploration trip to see the expanse of desert sand dunes and mountains of the Empty Quarter. A scorching hot sun tested the stamina of Bertram as he journeyed along with the much more experienced Arab Bedouin guides. The heat rising up from the sands would generate winds that circulated between high cliffs as they walked through a valley one afternoon. A whistling drone of a musical note began to come into hearing range one afternoon that seemed to emanate from a sand stone cliff not far away. The "singing sand" that he had heard of was giving its call to the weary travelers.

The constant blowing of wind carrying particles of sand would many times slowly ware away funnel shaped areas in the surrounding sandstone cliffs creating these wonders of sound in the wilderness. He looked in vain as they slowly made their way through the valley not seeing any such landform. The phenomenon remained unexplained.

Continuing daily for 9 or 10 hours each day they only stopped for sleep or to let their camels forage on infrequent patches of scrubby bush. On a distant hill there appeared images of three animals grassing in brush, the heat rising from the desert floor made their images wavy and not quite discernible. Only the tall spiraling horns occasionally showing as one of them raised its head indicated gazelles foraging in the distance.

Thomas and his party passed beyond an area of rose red colored sand and entered an expanse of white sand. It was, he wrote "a scene of utter desolation, a hungry void and an abode of death to whoever should loiter there." Just as he came to love the sand in its array of colors and forms, so he learned to fear it. At one point their party came upon what appeared to be a smooth salt plain but was instead a dry powdery quicksand capable of swallowing the entire length of a six-fathom plumb line.

Thomas learned too that the sand can be lethally treacherous when his guide recalls a tragic incident from memory. Pausing at a well, he was told by the tribesman that "four of my brothers lie in the bottom there. Two of them hand descended to clean it out and were overwhelmed by slipping sand, and their companions, following to rescue them were engulfed too. The well is a tomb. We have abandoned it."

After two months, of slow bone weary travel, Bertram Thomas and his companions emerged from the desert at the town of Doha on the Persian Gulf. He had covered more than 600 miles, and he had become the first westerner to cross the Rub'al Khali. Thomas' fear was soon matched by two other intrepid British explorers, Harry St. John Philby in 1932 and Wilfred Thesiger in 1947.

Reprinted by permission of Time Inc., publishers of Time Life books.

The Arabian Desert covers an area of 2,330,000 square kilometers (900,000 sq. mi.). The desert areas of Saudi Arabia have some of the largest expanses of sand dunes the size of ships, some dunes reaching up to 800' in height. Desert wildlife that roams these extreme climate areas includes the sand cat, Arabian Oryx, Gazelles, and spiny-tailed lizards. The climate is extremely dry with temperatures ranging from extreme heat to seasonal freezes at night. The ecology of this region supports only sparse biological diversity such as an occasional growth of scrub brush that nourishes any wandering gazelle

The striped hyena, jackal and the honey badger have gone extinct from this challenging environment. The sands of this immense desert area are made up of predominately silicates, composed of tiny granules of 80% to 90% quartz and the remainder feldspar, whose iron oxide coated grains color the sands in orange, purple, and red.

Today there is land disturbance caused by off road driving, and oil well expansion causing habitat destruction. Water well locations dot the landscape with circular sprinklers watering green circular patches of farm crops in various locations. The large remaining expanse of rocky mountain areas remains undisturbed except for the rare remote villages. The mountains and valleys with their various rock formations are what God has used to make all of the gigantic image scenes you will see that are covered in this book. For centuries the country of Saudi Arabia was considered closed to non Muslim outsiders and today it only continues to exist in the minds of the few vacation travelers willing to risk traveling there.

Unsettling news to my wife and myself

It was a startling and unsettling realization to both my wife and I, when she was diagnosed with uterine cancer. A trial of which my wife Mary encountered with trepidation and uncertainty. My love for her intensified, giving all the love and consolation through all the testing and treatments seem to calm the unexpected storm. There was a certain resilience in her character in this early time of malignant discovery, our faith was high in Father Gods control of the matter. The Holy Spirit is our comforter in whom we know and trust.

I remember telling her "sweetheart, I have heard encouraging words from your specialist and surgeon. When the time arrives that they determine the surgery to remove the affected area can be done, it will be taken care of." A gentle smile of reassurance crossed her face before I kissed her on the cheek and turned off the lamp beside our bed.

A sigh of relief for both of us came when the results of the lymph node testing showed no further spread of the cancer. The surgery was planned and that was a certain good sign.

A time of growing my faith of protection for the love of my wife during this period of time established a sense of stronger bonding between us. I desperately wanted to be there for her, and yes, she knew it and this comforted me.

Mary's surgery date came four weeks latter. Her apprehension was tempered with thoughts of "let's just get it over with." Her confidence gave me encouragement in giving her the best loving support in this uncomfortable place in our life, we knew our prayers would be answered. She recovered strongly and lived five more years.

CHAPTER 4
'The Throne of God & 'The Whole Duty of Man

Jeremiah 17:12 *A glorious high throne from the beginning is the place of our sanctuary. O Lord, the hope of Israel, all that forsake thee shall be ashamed, and they that depart from me shall be written in the earth, because they have forsaken the Lord, the fountain of living waters, KJV.*

Also see II Corinthians 5:10 *For we must all appear before the judgement seat of Christ; that every one may receive the things done in his body, according to that he hath done , whether it be good or bad, KJV.*

The portion of scripture underlined above is now revealed for fulfillment.

The Throne of God scene is very prominently seen at the following coordinates: 17 degrees 33'57.45"N 43 degrees 23'44.08"E Elevation 7139 feet, Eye Altitude 38,089 feet. Depicted here you will see the Throne of God, Jesus sitting at the right hand of the Father on his throne, the twenty and four elders, four beasts near the throne, a being holding two images one in each hand, and an image of a young man and lady running away from the throne. Yes, that is a lot of detail, and it is all there plain to see made up of the mountains and valleys of the location.

If you look closely at the image of God on the throne you will see a yellow fire in front of the left side of the face and within that there is a small scene. That scene looks like it could be a man and woman and a person standing in front of them holding a black book. If you will now look at the image of the young man and woman that are running away, what do you see? The young man is wearing pants… so he is of our modern day era. He is holding his right hand up covering his right ear as the young lady try's to talk to him. Ok, now look at the being that is standing with arms stretched out holding an image in each hand.

In the left hand, if you will zoom in and look at it closely you will see the following. There is the young man with his head lying on an open book. It looks like he is wearing glasses. Isn't that amazing, it is as though this has been prepared for today in our time for it to be revealed for our viewing and understanding.

Throne Room

There are only two scripture references in the whole bible that specifically address study, they are direct and to the point. In *II Timothy 2:15 Study to show thyself approved unto God, a workman that needeth not to be ashamed, rightly dividing the word of truth, KJV.* And in Ecclesiastes 12 :9-14 And moreover, because the preacher was wise, he still taught the people knowledge, yea, he gave good heed, and sought out, and set in order many proverbs. The preacher sought to find out acceptable words: and that which was written upright, even words of truth. The words of the wise are as goads, and as nails fastened by the masters of assemblies, which are given from one shepherd. And further, by these, my son, be admonished: of making many books there is no end; and much study is a weariness of the flesh. Let us hear the conclusion of the whole matter: Fear God, and keep his commandments: for this is the whole duty of man. For God shall bring every work into judgement, with every secret thing, whether it be good, or whether it be evil, KJV.

Now, please look at the image in the right hand of this tall being. To the best I can see it looks like a woman that has a scarf tied around the lower half of her face.

As we see thus far, comparing the only scriptures on study, can we discern this to be a husband and wife in ministry? It seems that the young man does not want to hear what his wife has to say in the matter. As a believer with our faith in Christ we all have a ministry. Whether it be an official capacity in a church or as a mother, father, student, etc. Has he and his wife chosen to run away from ministry? Has this young man chosen to not listen to his wife who may be trying to encourage him and work with him in ministry? What does this huge picture say to you?

What is God saying to the world by this huge mountain rock formation along with all the others? As we continue to look at the various images in this scene please look at the base of God's throne. See the people there? *Revelation 3:21 To him that overcometh will I grant to sit with me in my throne, even as I (Jesus) also overcame, and am set down with my Father in his throne, KJV.*

Also in *Mathew 20:23...but to sit on my right hand, and on my left, is not mine to give, but it shall be given to them for whom it is prepared of my Father, KJV.*

Do you see Jesus sitting on his throne to the right of the Father looking through a book? Is this the book of life that Jesus refers to in Revelation 3:5? As we look to the right of Jesus we see several people as though arranged similar to jurors at court. In order to have understanding of this we must go to *Revelation 4:4 And round about the throne were four and twenty seats: and upon the seats I saw four and twenty elders sitting, clothed in white raiment; and they had on their heads crowns of gold, KJV.* What other scripture can we refer to that will give any more information about this group? If we remember Peter's question to Jesus in *Mathew 19:27 …behold, we have forsaken all, and followed thee, what shall we have therefore? And Jesus said unto them, Verily I say unto you, that ye which have followed me, in the regeneration when the Son of man shall sit in the throne of his glory, ye also shall sit upon twelve thrones, judging the twelve tribes of Israel, KJV.* So we know that 12 of these 24 are the apostles of Christ.

What other scripture's shed more light on this heavenly scene? If we go to Psalms 82 beginning with verse *1 God standeth in the congregation of the mighty; he judgeth among the gods. How long will ye judge unjustly, and accept the persons of the wicked? Selah. Defend the poor and fatherless: do justice to the afflicted and needy. Deliver the poor and needy: rid them out of the hand of the wicked. They know not, neither do they understand; they walk on in darkness: all the foundations of the earth are out of course. I have said ye are gods; and all of you are children of the most high. But ye shall die like men, and fall like one of the princes. Arise, O God, judge the earth: for thou shalt inherit all nations, KJV.*

In verse one he says he judges among the gods. And in verse 6 please note that when God refers to man that he has chosen to sit near his throne they are spelled with a little 'g', gods, children of the most high. In verses 2 through 5 God speaks out to us here on earth that pervert justice by accepting persons of wicked character… that are in positions of leadership, thus perverting justice. We are to protect the poor and needy and prevent them from being taken advantage of, prevent treatment of cruelty and usery.

The wicked of the earth do not understand what is just. They are in darkness and do not understand compassion, love and blessing. The foundations are out of course. In I Corinthians 3:11…let every man take heed how he buildeth thereupon. For other foundation can no man lay than that is laid, which is Jesus Christ, KJV.

Now, let's consider the accurate time of this scene of the Throne of God. There are two appointed times of judgment. The first is for all Christians to stand in judgment for what we have done for Christ in this life. Romans 14:10-13. This is the judgment scene that we are looking at here. The other is the Great White Throne judgment which is only for the lost unbelievers who are presently in hell but will be judged at that judgment which is not included here.

Since we see the tall figure holding both arms out from the body with an image in each hand… Do you think this being may be a representation image of the 'Holy Spirit'? Jesus has told us in John 14:26 that when he left the earth his Father would send the Holy Spirit . John 14:26 *But the Comforter, which is the Holy Ghost, whom the Father will send in my name…KJV.*

Continually throughout our lives we face various difficult situations and good opportunities. Only by the written word of God can we determine factual basis upon how to view what we are seeing. By looking to the following scriptures we can know that God tries the hearts of men and he judges righteously each and every situation. *Jeremiah 11:20 But, O Lord of hosts, that judgest righteously, that triest the reins and the heart,…KJV.*

I Chronicles 29:17 I know also, my God that thou triest the heart, and hast pleasure in uprightness,…KJV.

Jeremiah 17:10 I, the Lord, search the heart, I test the conscience, even to give every man according to his ways, and according to the fruit of his doings.

Psalms 6:9 Oh let the wickedness of the wicked come to an end; but establish the just: for the righteous God trieth the hearts and reins.

Psalms 11:5 The LORD trieth the righteous: but the wicked and him that loveth violence his soul hateth, KJV.

James 1:12 Blessed is the man that endureth temptation: for when he is tried, he shall receive the crown of life, which the Lord hath promised to them that love him. Let no man say when he is tempted, I am tempted of God: for God cannot be tempted with evil, neither tempteth he any man: But every man is tempted, when he is drawn away of is own lust, and enticed.

Then when lust hath conceived, it bringeth forth sin: and sin, when it is finished, bringeth forth death, KJV.

So we know thus far that God tries our hearts and invokes us to do what is righteous (the will of God). Only evil brings temptation to do things that are wrong, hurtful, greedy or immoral. These scriptures and many others establish doctrine of true Christians that seek to live holy righteous lives.

By self- examination we know if we are true Christians if we have placed our full faith in Jesus and have turned away from any sinful lifestyle.

John 10:7-11 Then said Jesus unto them again, verily, verily, I say unto you, I am the door of the sheep. All that ever came before me were thieves and robbers: but the sheep did not hear them. I am the door: by me if any man enter in, he shall be saved, and shall go in and out, and find pasture. The thief cometh not, but for to steal, and to kill, and to destroy: I am come that they might have life, and that they might have it more abundantly. I am the good shepherd: the good shepherd giveth his life for the sheep, KJV.

How will we be judged?

You may be asking yourself "what specific scriptural references can I examine to know how I will be judged on what I have done as a Christian?" Please read Jesus's parable example in Luke 19:11-28. This is the parable given by Jesus that tells of a Kingdom Ruler (nobleman) that had received a kingdom in a far country for himself and returned there, Jesus is speaking of himself. Jesus tells us that before he had left that Kingdom in the beginning he had called together his servants and he gave them each one pound and told them to occupy till I come. Jesus wanted them all to occupy themselves with increasing what he had given them. However, there were those that did not like the imposed declaration of their ruler, saying "we will not have this man reign over us." Upon his return, he finds the rulers of this Kingdom, and he commanded that these servants be brought before him of whom he had given the money so that he could see how each had gained by trading.

The first servant said "Lord the pound that you gave me has made 10 pounds." Then the ruler said "Well done good servant, because you have been faithful with very little you will have authority over 10 cities." The second said "The pound you gave me has earned 5 pounds" The ruler said "You will have authority over 5 cities." The third person came up and said "Here is the pound that you gave me, I have it here wrapped in a napkin because I feared you, knowing that you are an austere man reaping where you had not sowed." The ruler answered "Out of your own mouth you are now judged by your own words, you wicked servant. You knew that I picked up that I had not lay down and reaped where I had not sowed. Why didn't you at least take it to the bank so that when I came back I would have my pound and interest earned also? He then said to those standing by take from him the pound and give it to the person having 10 pounds"

In this parable we see the servants of Christ. Every Christian is given according to our ability. Please read another account of this same parable in Mathew 25:13-30, in this account of the same parable Jesus tells the faithful servants "you have been faithful with a little now you will rule over 10 cities and the next servant you will rule over 5 cities. This gives example of what reward comes to the faithful after Jesus considers our work on earth. According to our abilities God has blessed us with what we have needed of and in the amount we can handle. We have free will to do what we want to do, however, what we do; say or think will be taken into account. Good works are a product of a Christian's life after he or she has accepted Jesus. Talents and gifts are given to us as well as a desire put into us to serve and we should never let the worldly cares of this world deter us from doing what is right, honest and good.

I remember an occasion when I was traveling and I stopped late one night to get a quick meal at a fast food shop. It was about 9:15 that night so they had only enough time to get that one hamburger prepared before cleaning the grill for the night. I was sitting eating my meal listening to the music that was playing and I saw a large silver Cadillac driving into the parking lot. The nicely dressed couple got out of the car and walked into the restaurant and began looking over the menu that was displayed above the counter. The elderly lady behind the counter said "I'm sorry but the grill has already been cleaned we're getting ready to close." The two people took this as an insult and said a few sharp words and then asked the elderly lady for her boss's phone number so they could call and complain the next day, then they turned and walked out. I quickly finished my meal, left a tip, and walked over to the nice elderly lady standing behind the counter and told her what a fine meal it was and how I admired her handling of the situation. I asked her for her boss's phone number also so I could call her boss the next day and tell him what a nice valuable employee he had. I knew that she could not ask her young teenage workers to work over time to prepare one more meal and she was very polite to the couple that wanted to be unreasonably demanding.

Sometimes you and I have opportunities to completely re-direct things that are evil onto a path that is good, honest and blessed. There are all sorts of opportunities out there for you and I to deposit something good into someone's life and sometimes these can seem very small or insignificant to us but actually they are more valuable than we imagine.

The main intent of the two accounts of the parable given by Mathew and Luke about the one talent and the one pound given to each servant is our level of dedication to use what God has given us in this life. We should want to use these gifts to the very best of our ability and be found faithful in doing so.

The scene that God has expressed in this picture is of two people running from God. If there are desires in your heart to serve God, by all means please devote time toward developing that desire. In my first experiences in teaching Sunday school at an early age I felt inadequate. Yet I persevered. I devoted time to prayer and study. Thoughts would come to my mind that I was not going to succeed. I latter realized these thoughts were from satan. If you will be patient in your pursuit whatever it may be and ask God to give you affirmation that what you are doing is working he will let you know from time to time through encouraging words from people. No matter what it is that you are doing if it is mowing the grass on the Church property, doing janitorial duties for the Church or visiting sick or elderly people, please do it with a loving heart and know that it is greatly appreciated. Please don't run away from it as shown in this picture.

One of my personal goals that I have accomplished in life is to encourage older men and women to volunteer themselves for at least 15 minutes to one hour to share a life story of their own with a Sunday school class of young people. Our young people do not all grow up hearing special personal stories of life that could help mold their minds toward living within the Grace of God. There are countless life stories within many people of how God brought them through a difficult time and blessed them. There are many kids growing up today in a single parent home that are missing out totally in having such revelations that impart wisdom. And not every family with children is going to experience the exact same circumstances in life, so the sharing of life stories benefit many.

So many kids today grow up only learning math, English, history, sports, etc. but when it comes to learning valuable living skills that are not academic… our educational structure falls short. I can think of one life principle that much of the time falls short in our modern system of education and that is interactive people skills and situation analysis. Of course in elementary levels children are taught something called citizenship but this is very basic, be polite, quiet, obey pedestrian rules when walking to school, etc.

The general consensus among educators when it comes to older children is that they will learn from each other as to how to interact with one another and they will learn such things as respect, integrity, trust, etc. from their parents or church. Those that don't learn valuable life lessons of how to interact with one another as well as identify critical matters in situations will find themselves in difficult situations later in life, some paying terrible costs such as jail time or missed opportunities for success.

Think about this for a moment in a slightly different way, let's say you're 50 years old, would you want to be judged by who you were 30 years ago at age 20 today? No, most likely not. Let's say you're 50 years old with a job that requires considerable responsibility, would you be as successful if you thought and acted the same as 30 years ago at age 20? No, most likely not. As a man thinks… that reflects who he really is. Absolutely everyone will make some mistakes in life but many are avoidable. We base our decisions on thoughts collected in our memory that form patterns of reasoning. Hopefully all of the many revelations of fact collected here about Christianity in these huge land base pictures that God has created will help you develop a deeper understanding of God.

The Scenes of Baby Jesus

Isaiah 7:14 Therefore the Lord himself shall give you a sign; Behold, a virgin shall conceive, and bear a son, and shall call his name Immanuel, KJV.

Ok, please go to your satellite earth view where you were viewing the scene of Abraham and Isaac sacrifice. Go directly left and down from there to the land of Aseer. To my absolute amazement I have found five individual scenes that all center around the theme of the birth of Christ. There is baby Jesus in the manger with Joseph looking down on him and several people around wearing turban head coverings and light colored garments, see coordinates 19 degrees 01'21.41"N 43degrees 01'42.74" E elevation 5134Ft., eye altitude 69 miles. It is very likely that most of these people had come with the wise men. There is strength in numbers when carrying valuable wealth with them as they did. Directly above this scene you can see angels looking downward upon the scene below. Right next to this scene to the right in a valley between mountains you will see Joseph kneeling down against a treasure chest with his hands on his head and Mary stands nearby holding baby Jesus in her arms as she looks on. They just received word that King Herrod had given the decree to kill all the male children two years old and younger. See coordinates 19egrees 05'31.21"N 43degrees 19'16.73" E elevation 4651 miles, eye altitude 19.70 miles. Directly above this is a scene showing two of the Wise Men discussing something and handing Mary something into her hands. Notice the size of the large jewel hanging on a necklace of one of the wise men! This particular scene is very dark in color and really takes your devoted attention to detail to see it. Coordinates 19degrees 10'01.89"N 43 degrees 15'32.24" elevation 4834Ft., eye altitude 14.38 miles.

Directly over to the right of the Bethlehem manger scene you will see another manger scene as a close up view, with baby Jesus in the circular manger, a baby lamb in the manger also with its neck raised up looking out, also a goat standing nearby, Joseph is kneeled down with his head bowed praying right beside the manger, see coordinates 18degrees 55'.56.26" N 43degrees19'53.47"E elevation 4891Ft., eye altitude 36.38 miles. And immediate to the right of this you will see baby Jesus being held up by Joseph. Mary is looking on smiling. You will see baby Jesus with his arms and hands stretched out in a playful way, see coordinates 18degrees 55'N 43degrees 42' E, elevation 4537Ft., eye altitude 50 miles.

THE SIGN OF CHRIST

Disciple healing baby

These images of stone and sand the size of mountains have been there for eons of time. Many miles across in size, they show the ware of time with soft visible lines of their shape and detail. Between the manger scene and this scene of baby Jesus being held up you will need to look lower down between these two scenes to see the scene of a king sitting down at a court meeting and there is a man small in stature with a turban on his head looking up at the king. It looks as though this could be king Herrod getting the news that a King has been born and the Wise Men have made their visit there. And this was the beginning of the second holocaust when he gave the decree to kill all the baby male children two years old and younger. The first holocaust was when baby Moses was born with a destiny to bring all the Hebrew people out of slavery from Egypt into the Promised Land. Scripture references for the birth of Christ begin with Mathew 1:18-25 and all of chapter 2. Let's look at verse 23 of Mathew chapter 1 *Behold, a virgin shall be with child, and shall bring forth a son, and they shall call his name Immanuel, which being interpreted is "God with us", KJV.*

From the beginning God's plan was to bring his only son "Jesus" to us for redemption. The very earliest scripture pertaining to this is *Genesis 3:15 And I (God) will put enmity between thee (Satan) and the woman, and between thy seed and her seed; it shall bruise thy head, and thou shalt bruise his heel, KJV.* The Holy Spirit would plant the birth of Jesus in Mary (woman's seed) bring God as man into the world to propitiate (substitute) the blood sacrifice for mankind. Please note that the original Hebrew says "HE will bruise your head" …this is 'Jesus". In a previous chapter we covered the blood covenant. God placed the blood covenant sacrifice into mankind to bring us into understanding the blood sacrifice made of 'Jesus', the once and for all time only sacrifice for the sin of mankind. I heard it said best once that God was showing us what extreme measure he was taking for us to show how much he loves us.

In Luke 1:26 And in the sixth month the angel Gabriel was sent from God unto a city of Galilee, named Nazareth. To a virgin espoused to a man whose name as Joseph, of the house of David; and the virgin's name was Mary. And the angel came in unto her, and said, Hail, thou that art highly favored, the Lord is with thee: blessed art thou among women. And when she saw him, she was troubled at his saying, and cast in her mind what manner of salutation this should be.

And the angel said unto her fear not, Mary: for thou hast found favor with God. And, behold, thou shalt convieve in thy womb, and bring forth a son, and shalt call his name JESUS.

He shall be great, and shall be called the son of the highest: and the Lord God shall give unto him the throne of his father David: And he shall reign over the house of Jacob forever; and of his Kingdom there shall be no end. Then said Mary unto the angel, how shall this be, seeing I know not a man? And the angel answered and said unto her, The Holy Ghost shall come upon thee, and the power of the Highest shall overshadow thee: therefore also that Holy thing which shall be born of thee shall be called the Son of God, KJV.

Please read all of the scriptures going forth from here. I am only pulling some of these scriptures pertaining to the picture images we are looking at. You are sure to see many more picture images within these mountain ranges as there are so many I couldn't possibly cover all the information in one book. In *Luke 2:6 And so it was, that, while they were there (in Bethlehem) the days were accomplished that she should be delivered. And she brought forth her first born son, and wrapped him in swaddling clothes, and laid him in a manger; because there was no room for them in the inn.* Let's look at verse 23 of Mathew chapter 1 Behold, a virgin shall be with child, and shall bring forth a son, and they shall call his name Emmanuel, which being interpreted is, 'God with us'. The very earliest prophetic hint is given to us in *Genesis 3:15 And I (God) will put enmity between thee (satan) and the woman, and between thy seed and her seed; it shall bruise thy head, and thou shalt bruise his heel, KJV.*

The Holy Spirit would plant the birth of Jesus in Mary (woman's seed) bringing God as man into the world to propitiate (substitute) for mankind. Please note that the original Hebrew says "HE will bruise your head"…this HE is 'Jesus". In a previous chapter we covered the blood covenant. God placed the blood covenant sacrifice into mankind to bring us into understanding the blood sacrifice at the time of Jesus's crucifixion. The overwhelming dynamic here is this, God chose to use the most extreme measure possible to connect with us. Showing his love by coming down from heaven, living among us as a man and then to be sacrificed. *John 3:16 For God so loved the world, that he gave his only begotten son, that whosoever believeth in him should not perish, but have everlasting life. For God sent not his son into the world to condemn the world; but that the world through him might be saved, KJV.*

Simeon holding baby Jesus

So we've established the fact that Jesus was planned to be birthed into our earthly realm at the earliest point of prophetic scripture here in Genesis 3. In *Isaiah 46:9-10 ...I am God, and there is none like me, declaring the end from the beginning, and from ancient times the things that are not yet done, saying, my counsel shall stand, and I will do all my pleasure, KJV.* The birth of Christ is preceded by the birth of John. See Luke Chapter 1 for the purpose of preaching the soon arrival of Jesus. Luke chapter 2 tells us more about the birth of Christ. Another fascinating image is depicted in this desert region. And this one is that of Simeon in Luke 2 starting in verse 28 As he picked up Jesus in his arms, and blessed God and said Lord, now let thou thy servant depart in peace, according to thy word: for mine eyes have seen thy salvation. I've created a color picture of this site located at coordinate's 18degrees 21'45.44"N 43degrees 54'34.06"E, elevation 5958Ft., Eye Elevation 32.55 miles. An interesting fact about this entire land area where baby Jesus is shown is called 'Asir'. In verse 36 of Luke chapter 2 tells us "and there was one Anna a prophetess, the daughter of Phanuel of the tribe Aser; she was of great age," She had come into the temple as was her custom often to fast and pray and came in near the same time that Simeon was there when Mary and Joseph had brought baby Jesus in to be circumcised. She also suddenly realized this little one as the promised Messiah.

Aren't family pictures wonderful? Just think of it, God formed these large mountains and valleys to show his family baby pictures to share with us.

A plan of the enemy ultimately fails

I eventually reached a point of having a good collection of digitized video segments and now needed someone with experience in how to build a complete story line. The first person I met was instrumental in getting these done.

The very next person advanced the collection into a near workable format but yet lacked continuity. Again a lack of certain skill sets necessary to accurately put into continuity of flow. And I could sense a cloud of interrupting need for more money even though no good production of useful product was coming forth.

Then I made contact with someone that prospectively had the skills and understanding of what I was working on. I met him at a coffee shop to discuss and show him what we would be working with in my ministry. All during the meeting at the coffee shop he would be looking over my shoulder as if giving me the signal that he had important pending business. I inquired so as to accommodate to his time. I was astounded to hear him say "well actually, I don't think you can afford me!" This was early in the development of this project, and I had at that time several thousands of dollars available to me from my 401K that I was living on, but of course I wasn't going to say that. On top of this situation, is the fact that this gentleman who has the computer skill sets to get the job done is also a man of God, preaching the word of God and he and his wife had served as missionaries for a number of years over seas.

I was eager to get some video work accomplished so we arranged a meeting to get started. Upon our starting he quickly threw some things together, and yes I mean literally quickly threw them together faster than I could follow and the after result looked less than professional. And I paid him the agreed upon $750 dollars for the two hour session. All the way home I was regretting having spent Gods money for something not usable. Knowing that the love of money is the root of all evil, it just infuriated me, and astounded me that a man of God could see the discovery, and know what potential it had to affect so many people and do such a thing. I prayed and shed tears all the way home on the two hour trip.

Yet I continued to pursue someone, and pleaded with the Lord for access to the one individual that had the right heart and proper skills. A year later I met that very person, and the video you see on timeclockrevelation you tube is the result. I am very pleased with it, a very good likeness to what was needed all along. The evil forces of envy, love of money, greed, and deception has plagued numerous people around me. Yet, as for myself nothing seems to bother me as I go about the business of developing this wonderful work of God.

These encounters increased my sense of alertness to the cunning ways of satans influence. I knew from the outset that this would occur, however I was not ready for how these things would take place. It all has been a learning experience, I know Father God has allowed these things to grow me and to further prepare me for work to come.

There have been other experiences along the way, trying to disrupt, delay, derail, or try to end my work. I remember a strong prophetic man of God say to me, "I don't know what this pertains to, or what this is about, but they can- not take what is yours, their sceams and lies will not affect the promised outcome." "God has specific purpose on you, you are anointed and appointed"

I have to the best of my ability kept this work a secret to keep ideas of men from influencing, a point well learned.

One of the most difficult times in my life

Five years after her previous battle with cancer, my wife once again experienced a repeat of similarity. She went through the usual tests for breast cancer, and the results came back positive. All of our prayer warriors that I could contact were notified. She was immediately scheduled for surgery, the time came and the surgery was successful. The time of her chemo treatments started soon after. Her frail little body could not take the chemo. She was in intensive care for two weeks and then in a nursing home for two weeks before being released to go home. She went back to work at the local college and retired at age 62. We at that time decided to build our dream home to retire into. She happily made plans of how she was going to decorate thus and so, and I was happy to see her so happy about something encouraging. I relaxed into the joy that she felt.

Then one morning she was complaining of back pain and hallucinating badly. I immediately called 911 and she was rushed to the hospital. She was carefully looked after and ex-rays were taken, then placed in intensive car. Two days later, the doctor and care manager met with me and told me that she needed to be admitted to hospice care. I immediately knew what this ment, and broke into tears. A love of 40 years is not easily broken. I called on everyone I could for prayer on her behalf. My world was one of being by her side in hospice care for 16 days. I would come home and ry to rest and cry out my tears in prayer. My church was there for me, not having any children of our own, that of the church was welcoming to me. Making all the funeral arrangements by myself was difficult, I seemed to go through the tasks the best I could. I remember calling her cousin Chad and I could hardly get the words out. As I write this a flood of emotions come again to overwhelm, a marriage of 40 years is not easily broken, I must move on.

CHAPTER 5
'The Cross'

I Peter 3:18 For Christ also hath once suffered for sins, the just for the unjust, that he might be made the righteousness of God, being put to death in the flesh, but quickened by the Spiri, KJV.

The wooden cross on which Jesus was crucified has been an enduring symbol of Christianity. Please look at an area that is located between Al Aqiq and Ranyah, Saudi Arabia. The coordinates are 20 degrees 45'22.26"N 42 degrees 21'13.33"E Elevation 3,684', eye Altitude 104.66 miles. You will see three pictures from different angles that God has provided for us to see. You will also see one of the thieves that hung on a cross near Jesus. The thief on the cross and Jesus on a cross are both shown as if we are looking down from heaven above on them. Then there is a picture showing Jesus that has been taken down from the cross and leaning up against the cross dead and bleeding. The third picture is showing Jesus hanging with arms up but no cross showing (it could be covered in sand) and something that looks like a bird flying away from him (Jesus's spirit leaves as he gave up the ghost).

Long before Jesus was born, the prophet Isaiah spoke of Jesus, as God revealed this to him in Isaiah Chapter 53. As I stated earlier, the first verse of Isaiah 53 tells us about the big Left Arm that has a spike going through the wrist out in the desert near Ryad Saudi Arabia. Today, this scripture is revealed for us to see literally (a prophesy fulfilled.)

Isaiah 53:1 Who hath believed our report? And to whom is the arm of the Lord revealed? For he shall grow up before him as a tender plant, as as a root out of a dry ground: he hath no form nor comeliness; and when we shall see him, there is no beauty that we should desire him.

He is despised and rejected by men; a man of sorrows, and acquainted with grief: and we his as it were our faces from him; he was despised, and we esteemed him not.

Surely he hath borne our griefs, and carried our sorrows: yet we did esteem him striken, smitten of God, and afflicted.

But he was wounded for our transgressions, he was bruised for our iniquities: the chastisement of our peace was upon him; and with his stripes we are healed, (KJV).

Crucifixion scene one

THE SIGN OF CHRIST

Crucifixion scene Two

All we like sheep have gone astray; we have turned everyone to his own way; and the LORD hath laid upon him the iniquity of us all.

He was oppressed, and he was afflicted, yet he opened not his mouth: he is brought as a lamb to the slaughter, and as a sheep before her shearers is dumb, so he openeth not his mouth.

He was taken from prison and from judgement: and who shall declare his generation? For he was cut off out of the land of the living: for the transgression of my people was he striken.

And he made his grave with the wicked, and wih the rich in his death; because he had done no violence, neither was any deceit in his mouth, yet it pleased the LORD to bruise him, he hath put him to grief: when thou shalt make his soul an offering for sin, he shall see his seed, he shall prolong his days, and the pleasure of the LORD shall prosper in his hand.

He shall see of the travail of his soul, and shall be satisfied by his knowledge shall my righteous servant justify many; for he shall bear their iniquities.

Therefore will I divide him a portion with the great, and he shall divide the spoil with the strong; because he hath poured out his soul unto death: and he was numbered with the transgressors; and he bare the sin of many, and made intercession for the transgressors. There are several scriptures telling of the future arrival of Jesus, Isaiah 7:14, 9:1-2, 6, 42:1-3, 50:6, 61:1-3.

While Jesus was still with his disciples he said in *Mathew 20:17-19 And Jesus going up to Jerusalem took the twelve disciples apart in the way, and said unto them, behold, we go up to Jerusalem; and the son of man shall be betrayed unto the chief priests and unto the scribes, and they shall condemn him to death. And shall deliver him to the gentiles to mock, and to scourge, and to crucify him: and the third day he shall rise again, (KJV).*

We have these numerous scriptures and others that tell us long before the event that Jesus would suffer at the hands of his accusers and would be put to death (sacrificed). And there is the many very huge pictures in the desert miles across in size that show Jesus wearing a crown of thorns, Jesus on the cross, Jesus beaten and bleeding. God has brought special emphasis to his son Jesus for all the world to see and read.

The actual accounts of the crucifixion of Christ are found in Mathew 26:31-75, 27:1-66, 28:1-20, Mark14:27-72,15:1-20, Mark 22:47-71,23:1-56, 24:1-53, and John 18:1-40,9:1-42, 20:1-31.

Jesus was crucified during the observance of Passover. In Exodus 12 God spoke to Moses and Arron and told them to have each family to slaughter a lamb and put the blood of it over the door post of each home. Exodus 12:1-14. In verse 13 And the blood shall be to you for a token upon the houses where ye are: and when I see the blood, I will pass over you, and the plague shall not be upon you to destroy you, when I smite the land of Egypt, also verses 14-27. This event was prophecy of the future sacrifice of the Lamb 'Jesus' as the final once and for all sacrifice for all man-kind.

A tremendous emphasis on the suffering that Christ suffered at the time of his crucifixion is certainly a sobering realization to the extent of cruelty that Jesus underwent for us. We must equally realize the tremendous overcoming power he showed to us in his resurrection of Life overcoming death. This is the overwhelming single reason. As both God and man he came down to earth and allowed himself to go through a physical death. Overcoming death with life has been the transforming life giving character of our loving God that he wants you and I to have, the same eternal life after our physical body dies. In the 28th chapter of Mathew we see that Jesus met Mary Magdalene and the other Mary while they were on their way to Galilee as the angel had told them to go and prepare to see Jesus there. Jesus said to them in verse 10 Be not afraid: go tell my brethren that they go into Galilee, and there shall they see me. In verse 16 they all met at a mountain that they had planned to meet at Galilee. *In verses 18-20 And Jesus came and spake unto them, saying, all power is given unto me in heaven and in earth. Go ye therefore, and teach all nations, baptizing them in the name of the Father, and of the Son, and of the Holy Ghost: Teaching them to observe all things whatsoever I have commanded you; and lo, I am with you always, even unto the end of the world, KJV.* Also see Mark chapter 16. In Luke chapter 24 we are told that Jesus also came unto two of the apostles as they walked to Emmaus. Jesus walked near them and heard them talking and he asked them why they were sad? And Jesus admonished them for not remembering what the prophets had spoken of him and what manner of death he would suffer. Again Jesus met with the eleven apostles and encouraged them. Also John's account is read in chapters 20 and 21. In the first chapter of Acts verses 3-11. ...

being seen of them forty days, and speaking of the things pertaining to the kingdom of God, (KJV).

The apostles tell us that told them to take up their cross and follow him, Mat. 10:38,16:24, Mk.8:34,10:21, Lk.9:23, 14:27. *In Colossians 2:13-15 ...hath he Jesus quickened together with him, having forgiven you all trespasses; blotting out the handwriting of ordinances that was against us, which was contrary to us, and took it out of the way, nailing it to the cross; and having spoiled principalities and powers, he made a show of them openly, triumphing over them in it, KJV.* We do well also to remind ourselves daily as we remember this blessed promise.

If you are now in Google Earth looking at the scenes with Jesus on the cross you will now need to use your mouse to move your screen view upward to see what I will describe next. Please keep in mind that these

Picture's are not in chronological order just like the bible is not in chronological order either. These pictures of biblical events God is using to tell an over-all story pictorially. With this statement I am explaining why we are now moving from the scenes of the cross to scenes of the life of David.

From these scenes, going upward the life situations of men grow darker. Please read 1 Samuel 16:7-18 to know that David was chosen by God to be king through their priest Samuel. God instituted a close relationship between king and priest to rule over the nation of Israel. The nation of Israel was dependent upon both of these positions of authority, please read Deuteronomy 20:1-13. David was chosen by God after Saul was removed from being king because he did not do exactly as commanded by the Lord to remove wickedness totally, please read 1 Samuel 15:10-26. No pictures are provided.

When I saw this, it shocked my sense of understanding momentarily

The following discovery unsettled me when examining the crucifixion scenes. Although I know the use of symbolism in Jewish text mean certain things, I really did not expect to see any identifying sign such as this. Roaming the surface of the ground around the crosses, there is a large swine, a hog.- Ok, I thought, God must have placed this here to symbolize the character of the typical criminals who ended up here. But then it occurred to me, the many, many criminals and accused criminals executed there, these Roman soldiers were not going to dig graves, in that rocky soil every day! This astounded me! Swine, will eat absolutely any dead thing, no matter what it is. This is why it is considered detestable, repulsive creature. Of course the body of Jesus was taken down for buriel in a crypt, and came as back to life as Father God originally planned, conquering death with life.

As you know from scripture, David stole Uriah's wife and committed adultery with her and then conspired and had her husband Uriah killed See II Samuel 12. These were deliberate decisive sins that caused David to live in misery. Verse 10 says because of this 'Now therefore the sword shall never depart from thine house; David reaped what he had sowed. The child that was born from the adultery with Bathsheba died. Later, his son Ammon entrapped and rapped his sister Tamar. Also, David's son Absalom had his brother Ammon killed. And Absalom caused David much grief until finally Absalom was murdered.

Please keep all this in mind to realize why the life of David is shown there on the mountain tops. God is reminding us that man can not involve himself in sin and expect blessing on his life. Man cannot sow seeds of iniquity without correction from the Lord. God will not bless the unfruitful deeds of unrighteousness. Remember how Job prayed for his children? He asked God to forgive them if they had sinned. He prayed protection over them and offered sacrifices on their behalf.

Another interesting scene in the life of David is at this following location.

At coordinates 23 degrees 17'54.35 N 39 degrees42'40.83 E at elevation of 2,889' and eye altitude 14.65 miles you will see Saul inside a cave with some of his men, they are laying down with a fire near their feet. You can see Saul with a blanket over him while he holds his spear. Nearby you will see a large war shield leaning up against the wall of the cave. This is found in I Samuel 24:3 And he came to the sheepcotes by the way , where was a cave; and Saul went in to cover his feet...KJV

Next Scene

After David and Saul's life we must go to google earth and adjust the screen view upward to the following location nearby.

At coordinates 22 degrees 42'55.25 N 39 degrees 25'56.85 E Elevation 689' Eye Altitude 29.30 miles you will see the event of the Red Sea crossing. See Moses sitting on the bank of the Red Sea facing away with his arm raised toward the sea, Israelites going past trailing off on the floor of the sea and walking up the far side. There appears the face of Moses, the face of the Queen of Egypt and Pharaoh there as well. The Israelites followed Moses and departed Egypt leaving the life of bondage and crossed over toward the Promised Land.

Ok, you have seen the life of David and realize all the trouble caused by sin and strife. Now, we see a scene of Crossing over by divine guidance. God is using these series of scenes to form an ultimate over all messages to us.

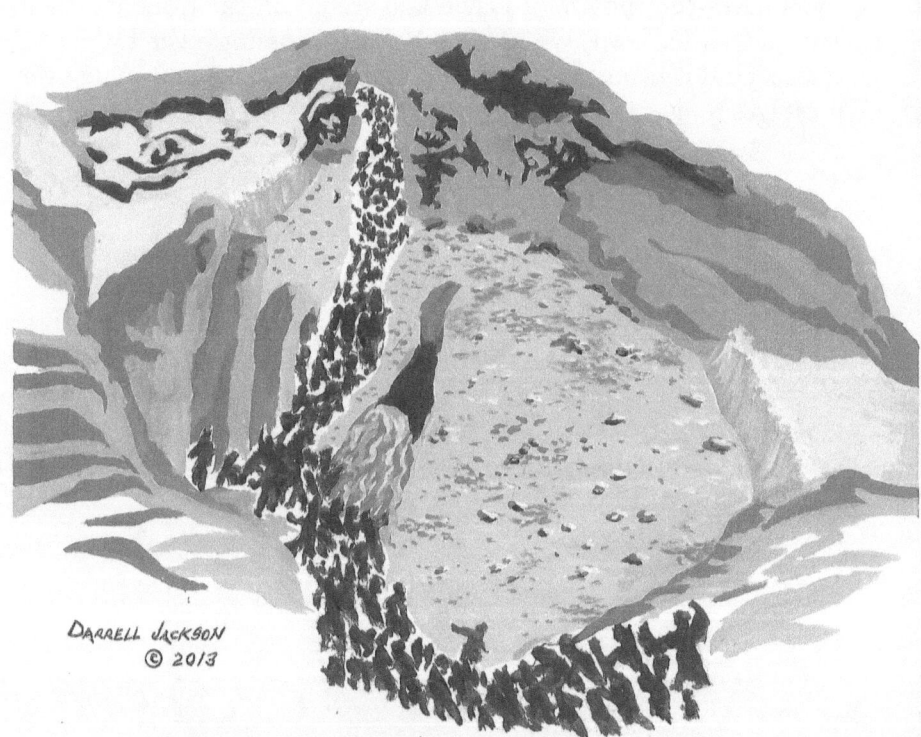

Moses at the parting of the Red Sea

CHAPTER 6
'The Good Shepherd'

Ok, let's stop here for a moment and reflect upon what God is trying to reveal to us thus far in order to put all of these scenes into pictorial story. First of all, the large continent of the Saudi Arabian Peninsula and Turkey that showed us Jesus our High Priest and King of Kings living, kneeling and praying for us. Next, the large left arm with the spike through the wrist and the Abraham & Isaac Sacrifice substitution with the picture of 'Jesus' with crown of thorns as the ultimate sacrifice to end the need for all other sacrifices. Then the 'Judgment Throne of God' and the people running away from God, then there is the birth of Jesus scenes. Next to that, the 'Jesus on the Cross' scenes are nearby. Then there is now the 'Red Sea crossing.'

First and foremost, God wants you and I to realize that Jesus who is our High Priest and King of Kings is the most important information communicated to us and he is fully in charge and that Jesus coming to earth was planned from the beginning of time. Jesus sits at the right hand of the Father at the throne now. God shows pictorial proof of Jesus birth and crucifixion as payment for the sin of man, if each individual person accepts Jesus. And now God is showing us the sinful beginning of David's life and now the crossing of the Red Sea.

This crossing represents people seeing an open escape path away from bondage. This crossing represents a decision to cross over and away from a life in bondage. God is telling you and I that all of man-kind has a decision to make, and in doing so it will determine your life pathway. Not to cross over away from a life of sin bondage leads into a picture area that is covered with pictures of demons and cruel war scenes in very dark colors of rock as well as small light colored areas. God had a plan set in place that gave the Israelites the opportunity to go into a promised land. Heaven is also a promised reward for those who follow Jesus. *Psalm 103:11-13 For as the heaven is high above the earth, so great is his mercy toward them that fear him. As far as the east is from the west, so far hath he removed our transgressions from us. Like as a father pitieth his children, so the LORD pitieth them that fear him, (KJV).*

When painting the picture of the Red Sea Crossing I had noticed that God placed pairs of eyes watching the procession going across the sea floor. And if you look closely, in one of the eyes, you will see the Egyptian kings face with long platted go tee.

Shepherds taking care of Lambs and sheep.

The way of salvation is sure. It is the way of Jesus. He will divide the waters for you. Express your realization that he rose from the dead and ask for the forgiveness of sins. By your realization that all of these huge gigantic pictures in the mountains and valleys speak a real message of God. It is all about Jesus.

At this red sea crossing site, if you follow the path upward where the Israelites cross over you will continually see pictures of sheep, shepherds and lambs all the way up the coast. These sheep, lambs and shepherds go all the way up to the shoulders of Jesus where they gather in a meadow. *Isaiah 9:6 For unto us a child is born, unto us a child is given: and the government shall be upon his shoulder: and his name shall be called Wonderful, Counselor, The mighty God, The everlasting Father, The Prince of Peace, KJV.* Ok, who is resting on his shoulders in this pictorial area you might ask? There are two clues... the sheep and the government. So who is the government? Please read *Revelation 5:9-10 And they sung a new song, saying, thou (Jesus) art worthy to take the book, and to open the seals thereof: for thou wast slain, and hast redeemed us to God by thy blood out of every kindred, and tongue, and people, and nation; And hast made us unto our God kings and priests: and we shall reign on the earth, KJV.* This refers to all peoples who have placed their faith in Jesus and they will be the reigning government during the millennium reign of Christ, our King of Kings.

So now that we see the restful location is under the headship of Jesus, on his shoulders... Jesus is the answer. Accepting the fact that Jesus has charge of you and I, if we accept his extreme sacrifice expressed in these miles of pictures. For scripture revealing our earned rest please read Hebrews 4:3-11.

We Christians who have died and gone on to glory will one day return with Christ to rule and reign with him on the earth in a peaceful magnificent way. Just imagine, our leadership being implemented without strife, stress, or any disagreement among management! What a wonderful restful way.

Jesus said in *John 10:7 Verily, verily, I say unto you, I am the door of the sheep. All that came before me were thieves and robbers: but the sheep did not hear them. I am the door: by me if any man enter in, he shall be saved, and shall go in and out, and find pasture. The thief cometh not, but for to steal, and to kill, and to destroy: I am come that they might have life, and that they might have it more abundantly.*

I am the Good Shepherd: the Good Shepherd giveth his life for the sheep. But he that is a hireling, and not the shepherd, whose own the sheep are not, seeth the wolf coming, and leaveth the sheep, and fleeth: and the wolf catcheth them, and scatters the sheep. The hireling flees, because he is a hireling, and cares not for the sheep, KJV.

In continuation of John 10 verse14, *I am the Good Shepherd, and know my sheep, and am known of mine. As the Father knoweth me, even so know I the Father: and I lay down my life for the sheep. And other sheep I have, which are not of this fold: them also I must bring, and they shall hear my voice; there shall be one fold, and one shepherd. Therefore doth my Father love me, because I lay down my life, that I might take it again. No man takes it from me, but I lay it down of myself, I have power to lay it down, and I have power to take it again. This commandment have I received of my Father.*

Jesus then had his disciples to be shepherds as well. In John 21:15-17 So when they had dined, Jesus said to Simon Peter, Simon, son of Jonas, lovest thou me more than these? He said unto Jesus, Yea Lord; thou know I love thee. He said unto him, Feed my lambs. He said unto him again the second time, Simon, son of Jonas, lovest thou me? He said unto Jesus Yea, Lord; thou knowest that I love thee. He saith to him, Feed my sheep, (KJV).

These words of Jesus set a standard for all shepherds (church pastors, evangelists, teachers, etc.) to continually feed their flock in the word of God. It is an absolute necessity for us to have our souls enriched with God's word regularly. The exact comparison of the duties of a shepherd of sheep can be compared to someone in a pastoral commitment. It is the duty to lead the sheep to green pasture, leading the flock into greater revelations of God's word, building up the strength of the sheep with additional wisdom and knowledge. All the while maintaining a constant watch, looking for danger that can creep into the flock to steel, kill and destroy. There are bitter herbs that grow among the grass where the sheep graze that can cause their milk to produce toxins that will harm their young ones who nurse that milk. It is the shepherd's responsibility to keep them out of these areas. Likewise, it is the responsibility of a pastor to keep sound doctrine of the bible always in reach of hungry souls. A pastor must watch for ravenous wolves that seek for someone to devour. This list would go on for several pages. We know of many things that exist in this world that would pull us away from our commitment to God. Sometimes a shepherd has to encourage sheep to come out of a barn where they are comfortable out into green pasture and to fresh water. Sometimes sheep want to settle for a stagnant pool of water but the shepherd knows that just over the next hill there is a clear stream of running water, living water that will sustain and refresh. Sometimes it is time for sheep to be encouraged into a barn to be protected from terrible storms of rain, hail, or snow.

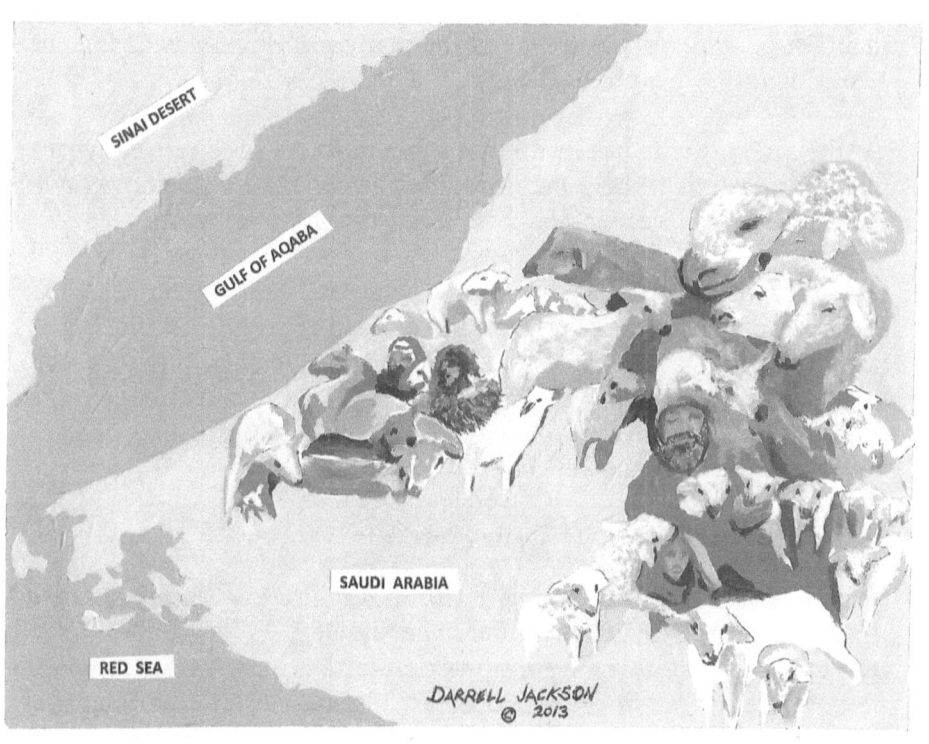

Shepherds and sheep gathered at Gulf of Aquqaba

Sometimes it is necessary for sheep to be nursed back to health with special attentive care. It is necessary at times for Christians to be under special attentive care of their pastor to receive compassionate advice, or compassion and prayer during a difficult health condition. There is a need at times to encourage people into a time of revival, prayer and fasting. And we all know that a sheep's coat of hair is course and very thickly matted. It needs to be sheered before hot summer. This wool makes it possible to warm and clothe many people as well as finance acquiring more sheep into the fold.

At the time my wife passed away, it was comforting and restorative for Christian friends to help me through it. It is not easy separating two people like our selves who have been married for forty years.

Today, if you are in a good church with a good Pastor who is a good shepherd of the flock then you and your family can learn much and grow spiritually and prosper well under such leadership. If that person of leadership follows and teaches all the love, wisdom and knowledge of Jesus then they are indeed giving to you out of the treasures of Jesus as we see in Colossians 2:2-3.

Jesus Pictures

During research within Google Earth in recent years I have seen new pictures emerge that I have waited to be revealed. As I have mentioned in previous chapters, there are times that sand is blown away to reveal new pictures and at times sand collects in places that show new pictures. You will now see some of these represented in this new updated book.

But first of all let's look at another fascinating mysterious feature that Father God has hidden in the Hebrew names in the very first generations of man. This has been known since at least the 1990's at its discovery time I think. Hebrew names have special meaning. These ten first generation Hebrew names are presented in Genesis chapter 5 beginning in verse one.

It is important to note that Cain and Abel's name do not appear, not mentioned at all because Cain killed Abel. Abel's life was cut short, not being able to accomplish any destiny. And evidently the murderous Cain did not have his name included for obvious reasons. This is why you see the recorded generational linage begin from Adam to son Seth. Now let's reveal the names and the original Hebrew meaning for each.

Adam	Man
Seth	Appointed
Enos	Mortal
Cainen (Kenen)	Sorrow
Mahalaleel	The Blessed God
Jared	Shall Come Down
Enoch	Teaching
Methuselah	His Death shall Bring
Lamech	The despairing (you and I)
Noah	Rest and Comfort

Placed together it reads: "Man (is) appointed mortal sorrow; (but) the Blessed God (Jesus) shall come down teaching (that) his death shall bring (the) despairing (you and I) rest!

Isn't it fascinating how Father God influenced the minds of those generations of parents to name their children in such a way. It is also interesting how Father God see's our earthly condition in the meaning of Lamech which is the root of "lamenting," synonymous with "despairing." This directly reflects back to our very need for the Savior "Jesus." As a noun it means: "A passionate expression of grief or sorrow." As verb: "To mourn a person's loss or death.) This is all of humanity's condition of the deep knowing of what was lost by Adam and Eve, the close daily relationship with God. This was only to be restored by Jesus dying for us on the cross.

The above mystery is a wonderful example of how God places a revealing trail of hints and scripture links for you and I to discover within these mysteries. It reveals his character, in how he lovingly gives all peoples of the world wisdom by such means. It is wisdom to search out the mysteries he has provided. Scriptures that speak of mystery's are: Mark 4:11, Romans 11:25, 16:25, I Corinthians 2:7, 15:51, Ephesians 1:9, 3:3, 3:4, 3:9, 5:32, 6:19, Colossians 1:26, 1:27, 2:2, 4:3, II Thessalonians 2:7, I Timothy 3:9, 3:16, Revelations 1:20, 10:7, 17:5, and 17:7.

Unlocking these mysteries, are only on Gods time table so that doors of our understanding are opened for us to advance into the next stage of His plan. We now are on a threshold of His kingdom advancement that is more glorious than we have ever imagined, please use it mightily to His glory. For ages we have been moving totally on faith without having to see visible proof, and today our faith soars with these God created pictures.

Jesus heals hearing

THE SIGN OF CHRIST

Jesus delivers maniac of demons.

Jesus heals blind Bartemaeus with spittle and mud.

THE SIGN OF CHRIST

Jesus stops stoning of woman.

A Wonderful Dream

While working on the God given assignment "The sign of Christ," I had a vivid dream that brought thankfulness to my heart, to know that I was right on time on God's time table. In retrospect I can see that it was Father God's encouraging intervening thoughtfulness in encouragement to my progress. In a peaceful sleep during an early morning hour of night, I had the following meaningful dream. There was a little baby in front of me, a cute little fellow. But there was something odd, something peculiar, on closer inspection of this little baby I see the difference. I brought my left hand around to his back and my right hand behind his head and tilted him closer to me. The baby had whiskers! A five o'clock shadow! And in the dream I said "You have a very nice beard. And the baby said "Thanks, you have a very nice beard too!" And I was surprised. Then I heard these words from the Lord "That which is in its infancy is having early maturity," and the dream ended. I was very encouraged, and laughed about the beard conversation before drifting off to sleep.

The Sword of the Lord

Island of Cyprus'

While looking at the area of the Mediterranean Sea just under Turkey you will see that the island of Cyprus is just a few hundred miles off the coast of Turkey. Please look at its location in regard to the whole image of Jesus kneeling and praying. You will see that it is just outward from the hidden face of Jesus not far away from where his mouth would be. What is significant about this? What is significant about the shape of the island of Cyprus?

We must refer to scripture to find the significance, scriptures that directly address this pictorial expression. *In Ephesians 6:17...and the sword of the spirit, which is the word of God; KJV* The word of God comes from the mouth of Jesus, it cuts through the clutter of man's foolish ideas. Doesn't it make sense that God created a book of directions, instructions that will enable man to live a life of wonderful freedom in joy and peace? Of course it also offends people when their sin is addressed as unacceptable before God and thusly it cuts. This is the only sword that cuts away terrible damaging things from a person's life and immediately causes healing. A surgeon's scalpel cuts away cancer from a human body when necessary for healing to take place.

However, it is not necessary for anyone to feel pain when giving up a sin of any kind. Jesus takes that which we give up and give to him and wipes it away as if it were never done. After he forgives us…we only need to forgive ourselves.

Hebrews 4:12 For the word of God is living, and powerful, and sharper than any two edged sword, piercing even to the dividing asunder of soul and spirit, and of the joints and marrow, and is a discerner of the thoughts and intents of the heart, KJV. The word of God is living and powerful in the sense that it is always relevant and revealing the mind of God. This very collection of pictures now being revealed thousands of years after he created them are testimony to this fact of scripture coming alive with modern day relevance!

When Jesus was out in the desert fasting and praying, satan came and tempted him. Satan said "if thou be the son of God just command that these stones be turned into bread". Jesus answered by quoting *Deuteronomy 8:3…that man doth not live by bread only, but by every word that proceedeth out of the mouth of the Lord doth man live, KJV".* This is an example of how Jesus used this sword. When facing conditions that are opposed to God we must refer to God's word.

What responsibility do those of us have in bringing forth the word of God to others? We must use as much scripture in explanation of scripture as possible. The word of God explains itself when thorough research is done on the subject being studied. A very cautious attention to this must be taken due to the consequences such as spoken by Jesus in *Mathew 13:19 When any one heareth the word of the Kingdom, and understandeth it not, then cometh the wicked one, and catcheth away that which was sown in his heart, KJV.* And in *verse 23 But he that received seed in the good ground is he that heareth the word, and understandeth it, who also beareth fruit, and bringeth forth, some an hundred-fold, some sixty, some thirty,(KJV).* Yes, thorough understanding must be established when teaching the bible.

Having the word of God abiding in us is extremely valuable in Gods expressed opinion, as we see as Jesus spoke to the Pharisees and Sadducees. Most of them did not have a sound understanding of the prophetic scriptures of the old testament that clearly identified Jesus. *John 5:38-39 And ye have not his word abiding in you; for whom he hath sent, him ye believe not. Search the scriptures; for in them ye think ye have eternal life; and they are they which testify of me, KJV. Again in verses 46-47 For had ye believed Moses, ye would have believed me; for he wrote of me. But if ye believe not his writings, how shall ye believe my words?(KJV)*

When the apostle Paul visited the village of Berea he makes note of their diligence in the word of God in *Acts 17:11 These were more noble than those in Thessalonica, in that they received the word with all readiness of mind, and searched the scriptures daily, whether those things were so, KJV.* And this necessary need of study is still with us today. As we read scripture on a regular basis, we retain much of it without realizing it as time progresses throughout our life. And at times we have those "ah ha" moments when something jumps out at us from scripture that we seem to discover for the first time as the spirit of God speaks to us through his word. These are valuable golden moments of inspiration born of God. This further illustrates how God's word is alive.

The word of God is permanent; it will never disappear from mankind. Jesus said in *Mark 13:31Heaven and earth shall pass away, but my words shall not pass away, (KJV)*. God's plan and purpose for man will always exist in recorded word for all eternity.

Jesus – The Word of God

In *John 1:1-5 In the beginning was the word, and the word was with God, and the Word was God. The same was in the beginning with God. All things were made by him; and without him was not anything made that was made. In him was life; and the life was the light of men. And the light shineth in darkness; and the darkness comprehended it not.* See also John 1:14 – the Word became flesh and dwelt among us. Also *John 17:5, John 1:10, I Corinthians 8:6, John 5:26, 8:12, 11:25*. Jesus is the full embodiment of the fully expressed word of God. The total expression of all righteousness, since Malachi 3:18 clearly states righteousness is the total will of God and how we serve God, thusly the all complete 66 books of the bible. And in the second sentence in this paragraph above in John 1:3 it states Jesus was there during the creation process, involved in the process. In Jesus there is life (verse 4) the light of men. Light that exposes truth, unveils mystery, states a fullness of expressed love for us to prosper.

And in verse 5 of John chapter one this light of Jesus shines through darkness. Eliminating darkness through Jesus is the always accessible way of Jesus. The last part of that verse tells us the darkness cannot comprehend the light of Jesus. Its plans are spoiled; its affect has no effectiveness to the Holy, Pure, Righteous Christian. These three attributes in the life of a Christian is the protective power that enables you to be the effective soldier being fully equipped as expressed in Ephesians 6:10-18, and II Corinthians 6:7 which states " by the word of truth, by the power of God, by the armor of righteousness on the right hand and the left."

CHAPTER 7
"The location of an image of HELL"

'Consequence of no decision'

John3:17-18 For God sent not his Son (Jesus) into the world to condemn the world; but that the world through him might be saved. He that believeth on him is not condemned: but he that believeth not is condemned already, because he hath not believed in the name of the only begotten Son of God, (KJV).

It is very important for me to point out that there is no scripture that explicitly says "Hell is in the earth," however, the scriptures that are identified here lead to that direction.

Now we must look at a terrible disturbing scene in the area of the Sinai Desert where a pictorial scene of Hell exists. This is not to say that this is where hell exists, it is a location on the surface of the earth that God chose to show a picture inside of hell. The dark areas that I mentioned earlier from Medina upward through Khaybar and to Tabuk which are terrible war scenes with facial pictures of demons lead upward to the area of the picture of hell. Please do not get the idea that I'm saying that anyone who finds themselves in military war are destined for hell. That is not being said at all. God is showing us by way of allowing the pictures of demons there to show us where war actually originates from. Sometimes as Christians we must defend our country by serving in the military to protect our way of life.

The war scenes are not plain to see. In fact you've really got to zoom in close and look for them, because God does not want to glorify war but he does want us to know where this influence comes from. Possibly in my next book I may show some of the war scenes.

Why did God use scenes of war you might ask? Within any war there exists practically every sin known to man. God is only using this to show us the depraved side of man if you decide to go that route in life. Those that choose to separate themselves from God will fall into sinful lifestyle and end up eventually in Hell. These war scenes are very small and dark and difficult to see because God does not want to glorify sin by giving it a prominent placement.

The pictorial area in the Saini Desert area that shows scenes of hell are located in the following location 29 degrees 51'00.16" N 33 degrees 53'29.30" E with 1552' elevation and eye altitude of 145.82 miles. This will give you an over- all view of this scene. These are included in the video at timeclockrevelation you tube. Within this you will see a full body of a man in a whirlwind of fire, a woman trying to climb up out of the pit and she is engulfed in flames. There are human skulls, demon faces and terrible looking creatures on fire. Notice right below the face of a large demon you see the face of Hitler. These are in the video to be seen in timeclockrevelation you tube. There is an elderly lady with a bee hive hair style and many wrinkles on her face. All of these are as though we are looking down at them from above. And if you go in to google earth at this location, zoom out and swing this whole image around upside down... you will see that the whole scene including everything forms what looks like one large demon climbing up out of a pit. If you look closely you will see many demonic faces everywhere within the area.

Nearby to this large picture of hell you will see a young man shown from the waist up shaking his fist and looking upward at 28 degrees 33'06.36" N 33 degrees 55'39.08"E and 5,128' elevation and eye altitude of 204.44miles.

What does God say about Hell? *Deuteronomy 32:22 For a fire is kindled in mine anger, and shall burn unto the lowest hell, and shall consume the earth with her increase, and set on fire the foundations of the mountains, KJV.* Also see Ezk.26:20. So we know by this that it is a place of fire, a place of anger, a very low part within the earth and it gradually increases in size as lava of the inner earth's magma churns and the earth's crust gradually moves in subduction. We see evidence of volcano activity, lava flow and earth quakes throughout time which explains how hell consumes the earth with its increase. *In verse 24 They shall be burnt with hunger, and devoured with burning heat, and with bitter destruction: I will also send the teeth of beasts upon them, with the poison of serpents of the dust. The sword without, and terror within, shall destroy both the young man and the virgin (those of youth that have reached an age of accountability and rejected God) along with the man of gray hairs.*

I said I would scatter them into corners, I would make the remembrance of them to cease from among men. Psalm 9:17 The wicked shall be turned into hell, and all the nations that forget God, KJV. If you will notice near the bottom of the picture of hell near to the Gulf of Aquaba you will see a woman dressed in black laying seductively on her side so as to seduce. This mountain sized picture is located at 29 degrees 40'54.79"N 34 degrees 44'14.70"E Elevation 2,369' Altitude 58.36 miles. In Proverbs 5:3-6 and Proverbs 7:5-27 these verses speak of harlotry, adultery, fornication that leads to hell. *Verse 27 her house is the way to hell, going down to the chambers of death.* Also Proverbs 9:13-18 speak to this same issue. Will hell ever be so full that no more can be added? No, *Proverbs 27:20 Hell and destruction are never full; so the eyes of man are never satisfied, KJV.*

Ecclesiastes 8:8 There is no man that hath power over the spirit to retain the spirit; neither hath he power in the day of death: and there is no discharge in that war; neither shall wickedness deliver those that are given to it.KJV At our time of death we have no control of our inner spirit body. If we have lived by our decision to keep ourselves separated from God then we will continue to be separated from God permanently. When such a spirit of a man leaves in death such as an atheist, even it's atheist friends morn that persons death. Because they know deeply that the spirit within that body whom they loved is not there any longer.

Where is hell? As previously mentioned by example, hell must be inside the earth. Hell is also referred to as the bottomless pit. The earth is a circular sphere like a ball, the inside of a sphere has no bottom, Revelation 9:1-2, 9:11, 11:7, 17:8, 20:1, 20:3. The interior of the earth at its core, there exists extreme heat, molten rock. Best estimates of temperature by scientific geophysical models arrive at a temperature from 9,000 degrees to 12,000 degrees Fahrenheit. The earth spins on its axis causing an internal centrifuge of high pressure. This extreme high pressure of weight and mass result in high inner core temperature and makes possible an electromagnetic field. This magnetic field emanates outward from the earth's surface out into space and shields the earth's surface from solar winds from the sun. Without this magnetic field shield it would not be possible for life to be protected from the extremely powerful solar flares.

Even just a few miles below us there are the beginnings of high temperatures. Many oil wells going to depths of four miles or more encounter high temperatures that require special operating equipment and procedures. Since we know that fallen angels have been placed in this containment area, it is definitely not a place that you should desire to go, a place of eternal darkness, hatred, fear and suffering for all of eternity. Please read Luke 16:19-25.

We must read the parable in Luke 20:9-18 to gain a greater understanding of how the threat of evil princes, fallen angels conspire and contrive in order to lead man into darkness to be destroyed. The best way for them to hide is for them to procreate the mith that they don't exist. This scriptural parable example is how they conspired against Jesus. Jesus gave this parable at the very beginning of their plotting against him long before he was crucified. However, these evil spirits were actually doing what God knew they would do. Jesus was intending to go to the cross and suffer death in order to prove his invincible ultimate power over death as his plan for the redemption of man. *Verse 9 Then began he to speak to the people this parable; A certain man (Father God, Jesus, Holy Spirit) planted a vineyard, and let it forth to husbandmen, and went into a far country for a long time, KJV.* God planted the vineyard of man-kind and set men to be responsible for the care of the vineyard of man-kind, Isaiah 5:1-7. Jesus, as planned, is to leave for a long time (from the time of creation until he arrives as birthed by Mary).

Verses 10-12 And at the season he sent a servant to the husbandmen, that they should give him of the fruit of the vineyard: but the husbandmen beat him, and sent him away empty. And again he sent another servant; and they beat him also and entreated him shamefully, and sent him away empty. And again he sent a third; and they wounded him also, and cast him out, KJV. Many servant prophets of God were sent into the vineyard of man to gather fruit…to gather and nurture God's people in the way of the Lord God Jehovah. They were treated cruelly, chased, beaten and some killed. At times the Jewish tribes had leadership that became corrupt and God could not bless their evil doings, they were conquered by their enemies.

Verse 13 Then said the Lord of the vineyard, what shall I do? I will send my beloved son: it may be they will reverence him when they see him. But when the husbandmen saw him, they reasoned among themselves, saying, This is the heir: come, let us kill him, that the inheritance may be ours, KJV. The evil princes of this world see Jesus arrive as heir to the throne in the body of a man and influence evil men in religious authority to kill him.

Verse 15 So they cast him out of the vineyard, and killed him. What therefore shall the Lord of the vineyard do unto them? KJV Jesus is explaining to those hearing him preach this parable about what was unfolding before them as he was preparing to soon go to the crucifixion of the cross. However, the evil princes of this world did as God knew they would and in effect made the ultimate act of Love by God possible without them realizing it 1 Corinthians 2:8. For God to come down among men and die a physical death then rise again and take all the old testament saints out of paradise (the fruit of the vineyard) onward up to heaven was miraculous.

Verse 16 He shall come and destroy these husbandmen, and shall give the vineyard to others. And when they heard it, they said God forbid, KJV. The old Testament form of temple worship ended. The care of the vineyard was given to the gentiles as the apostles of Christ Jesus spread the gospel outward unto the uttermost parts of the world. Please read Proverbs 1:24-31, John 1:11-13, Romans 11:11

Verse 17-18 Jesus then said "What is this then that is written, The stone which the builders rejected, the same is become the head of the corner? Whosoever shall fall upon that stone shall be broken; but on whomsoever it shall fall, it will grind him to powder." The stone that the builders (Sadducee's and Pharisee's) rejected was Jesus. For greater understanding of the corner stone please read Job 38:1-7, Psalm 118:20-23, Isaiah 28:16-18 and Mathew 21:42. Please know that evil demonic forces are still at work, please do not be deceived and fall into the traps laid for you.

Mathew 10:28 And fear not them which kill the body, but are not able to kill the soul: but rather fear him which is able to destroy both soul and body in hell, KJV. You don't have to go to this place. It is up to you to decide that you will give your heart and soul to Jesus and follow his direction. Do you want to be at peace with your life? God loves you very much. This is the reason that God has created these huge mountain pictures for us to see that matches bible scripture.

It is expected of us to seek God first before God will cleanse our life and make it whole. If you will pray in your own words "Lord Jesus, I come to you now and accept your love for me. I ask you to forgive me of my sins and come in to my heart, I want you to have my life".

Jeremiah 29:11-13 For I know the thoughts that I think toward you, saith the Lord, thoughts of peace, and not of evil, to give you an expected end. Then shall ye call upon me, and ye shall go and pray unto me, and I will hearken unto you. And ye shall seek me, and find me, when ye shall search for me with all your heart, KJV.

If you have prayed in your own words to accept Jesus and have meant this truly from your heart, then you have entered into covenant with God as one of his beloved children. You must follow God's word in your life so that you can live your life abundantly. If you were to die after doing this then your home is in Heaven. You have full reason to rejoice.

Please join a church where the complete word of God is taught and let that pastor know about the decision that you just made so you can be baptized. *John 5:24 Verily, verily, I say unto you, he that heareth my word and believeth on him God the father, that sent me, hath everlasting life, and shall not come into condemnation, but is passed from death unto life, KJV.* Please spread the news about this wonderful revelation of these picture signs that are now given to us. As a new believer you will have a desire to know more about God. God places this in our hearts so we can develop into the stronger Christian fully equipped.

After receiving Jesus you should devote time toward developing your knowledge and wisdom of Christ. What we think about during idle times tends to shape our outlook on life and this is the perfect time to grow spiritually continually. Please read Philippians 4:7-9, we know by these scriptural truths that the peace that God places in our hearts is far beyond our understanding. That inner peace is more wonderful than any you will ever experience.

When we meditate on the word of God we experience truth to the extent that we gain greater understanding of God's purpose and his love. The honesty and justice of God is much more far reaching than that of man. The purity of which God desires for you keeps our mind in a state that God can come into, giving life sustaining love, knowledge and wisdom. You will also be encouraged as you hear good reports from fellow Christians who receive blessings. These virtuous praises feed your soul and strengthen your spirit.

It is necessary for you to allow God to fully equip you. Please read Ephesians 6:10-18, in doing these things you will be strong in the power of Christ's might as it says in verse 10. If we tap into this statement to its fullest potential we can be assured of being fine Christian soldiers who will be ready for assignments in Gods Kingdom. We must put on the whole armor of God in order to stand against the wiles of the devil. For we wrestle not against flesh and blood, but against principalities, against powers, against the rulers of darkness of this world, against spiritual wickedness in high places (fallen angels). We must have the belt of truth, the true gospel of Jesus Christ, hold fast to these core principles of our faith. These pictures on earth that depict God's word I hope have strengthened your faith even further.

We must wear our breastplate of Righteousness, serving God, which is the will of God, Malachi 3:18 ...*discern between the righteous and the wicked, between him that serveth God and him that serveth him not, KJV*. As we know, the breastplate protects the heart. Let's stop for a moment and examine what 'the heart' is. The 'heart' is the core value that you place on any subject idea, our conscience. Depending on what value you have on any given subject, that value could be valuable truth or deceptive evil falsehood. God tests each one of us in this crucial area as we see in *Jeremiah 17:9-10 The heart is deceitful above all things, and desperately wicked; who can know it? I, the Lord, search the heart, I test the conscience, even to give every man according to his ways, and according to the fruit of his doings, KJV*. A fine example directive that King David gave to his son Solomon when David was dying on his death bed, read I Kings 2:3-4. In reading these two verses you will notice after telling Solomon to adhere to God's word, ...to walk before God in truth with all their heart and with all their soul. Do not allow deceitful wickedness to rule your conscience. Allow God's Word, love, statutes, commandments, his ordinances and his testimonies to rule your heart, (true righteousness).

And continuing with the armor we must wear in Ephesians chapter 6, we must have our feet shod with the preparation of the gospel of peace. Have you wondered why the feet are mentioned? Our feet take us where ever we go. When going out into the world we must have the word of God guiding our steps. The word of God can tell us where we are to move spiritually if we are seeking direction. And we read 'with the preparation of the gospel of peace'. All the good intentions you may have, if not done with proper preparation of study in God's word and preparation by prayer… without these… your good intentions fall short. The gospel of peace is from the Prince of Peace Jesus.

And above all as it says in *Eph. 6:16 Above all taking the shield of Faith, with which ye shall be able to quench all the fiery darts of the wicked, KJV.* Our faith constitutes absolute trust in God's love for us, his statutes, his commandments, his ordinances and his testimonies in his word. Nothing that wickedness sends toward us will separate us from God's love, Romans 8:38-39.

When you accepted Jesus as your savior (becoming a Christian) you placed a helmet of salvation upon your head so to speak. You must allow this act of faith that you express to God accepting his son Jesus to protect your mind. Many ideas of men contend with actual truth, posing contrary arguments that intend to come against your mind. Keep your helmet of salvation over your mind. Please take the sword of the spirit which is the word of God, your bible, and read daily to feed your spirit in ever increasing knowledge and truth. Hold strongly to righteousness protecting your heart from impure wicked imagination. To complete this equipping of armor we go to *2 Corinthians 6:7 … by the armor of righteousness on the right hand and on the left, KJV.* As we are about our daily business with our hands busy doing whatever tasks that are before us we should be doing all within the bounds of righteousness. And as stated earlier righteousness is serving God, doing the will of God Malachi 3:18.

A Very Meaningful Dream

Another dream that provided uplifting encouragement came at a very important time while taking care of my wife during her cancer treatments. As I look back, I now realize that God's timing is perfect within its intended season. The very pictures that I had been waiting to show up, pictures of Jesus's ministry, were just a few months ahead to be revealed by the blowing away of sand. This a very important fact that I had been waiting on for five years at this time. That my fellow Christian friends, is extremely important and now in 2018 I see the images in detail to include within the full breadth and scope of the message.

The dream that I had at that time was an incouragement dream with blessed meaningful intent. Within the dream experience at that time, it was a very awe inspiring dream message that propelled me into further work. Where much is given, much is required. As the dream message began, I was standing near a street intersection that intersected a railroad track within a city. I noticed at the edge of a street curb and under the edge of the railway, partially covered in sand were two brilliantly shinning objects. Just enough of the surface of the two objects was showing through the sand to attract my attention. I walked over, knelt down and brushed sand away with my hand. The first object was a thick round sold gold disk about 3" thick with all sorts of precious jewels adorning the top of it. The second object was also the same thickness of solid gold in a rectangular shap. On the top of it were stars and strips like our American Flag. Precious jewels adorned every star. The brilliant stripes were shinning with beautiful color. The expressed thought into my mind at that point was the following "The message images are very important and valuable to our united states and the world, our country spreads the gospel of Christianity more than any other country in the world." Our lord's moving the sand away to reveal, continues and it is of high value in revelation of who God is.

THE SIGN OF CHRIST

Holy fire no longer fails to consume sacrifice.

CHAPTER 8
"The Sounding of the Shofar"

The last pictorial scene is located within the bent foot of Jesus located directly to the right of the scar location on the foot in a mountainous area south of the city of Muscat. The picture is located at coordinates 22 degrees 47' 13.98" N 58 degrees 51' 45.98" E and best viewed at altitude of 94.80 miles. This is a picture of two persons, with only their heads showing. The one on the left is holding a Shofar to his lips as if blowing a trumpet call. The person to his left is in prayer as signified by his eyes being closed and hands held up to his face folded together. Personally, I believe these two people are real people that lived in time past as all of the people shown in these pictures we have looked at. If we believe Jesus's parables and he said a sower went forth to sow…then there was actually a sower of whom he was referring to. Jesus knew the many ways of man-kind and could tell of many specific people and what they had done, that is no surprise to us. Could it be possible that these two people are the two prophet witnesses mentioned in Revelation 11:3-12? Some Christian scholars say that these are Enoch and Elijah. I get goose bumps as I discover this pictorial sign and consider its significance. What I find significant about this is its location on the map. Please refer to the map drawing that shows all of the wounds that occurred to the body of Jesus.

Please consider this specific location, when a man's body is first placed onto a cross the first parts of his body to be secured would be the two arms. The last part of the body to be nailed to the cross would be the feet. It is not my intention to suggest any interpretation to these facts, only to point out such detail as it appears. So it appears that this trumpet call sign is the last in the series of pictorial signs because it is located all by itself way over near the nail scar of the feet of Jesus. Is God telling us something here? Interestingly enough, in systematic theology or bible doctrine we recognize eschatology (the study of last things) to be significant.

Trumpet about to be blown.

The most striking symbolic detail we see in this picture is the shofar being blown. In order to establish a firm understanding of this we must examine the purpose and usage of the shofar. I am by no means any expert in the knowledge of Hebraic implements of worship. An excellent source of documentation for my research has been a book titled "Jewish Faith and the New Covenant" by Ruth Specter Lascelle.

The shofar is the ritual ram's horn of the Hebrews, the oldest known form of wind instrument, which makes a sound similar to modern day trumpets. The ram's horn is blown as a summons to conscience to awaken and heed the call of duty. In biblical times the trumpet was used for various announcements, like that of the New Moon and Festivals (Psalm 81:3; Numbers 10:1-10; Isaiah 18:3) signals of alarms, summoning the people together, the call to battle, the stopping of pursuit, for dismissal of the army to return home, as a signal of victory, and as an instrument in processions. It was also blown at the offerings presented to the Lord, for proclaiming of an important event such as the accession of a ruler to the throne, and to make known the start of a fast.

My attention is drawn to the Jewish holiday of "Rosh Hashanah", "The Feast of Trumpets" to establish a greater understanding of possibly why this picture of the two individuals are there with seemingly no other purpose but to emphasize something significant. In the Old Testament it is not called by either of the two tittles mentioned above. In Leviticus 23:24 it is called "Zikhron Teruah" (Memorial of blowing [of trumpets]. Rosh Hashanah means "Head of the Year. After the destruction of the second Temple in the second century A.D. these two where considered one and the same. This is observed in the autumn of the year at the first day of Tishri, the seventh Hebrew month, which would be mid-September – early October. In Ezra 3:1-6 we see the only reference to this Feast being celebrated right after those returning from Babylonian exile had rebuilt the Temple Alter. Trumpets were blown at the beginning of this seventh month with long blasts to emphasize solemnity making it unique among months.

Another significant fact we need to consider is that Rosh Hashanah was sometimes referred to as "Yom Ha-Din ("Judgment Day"). The Shofar is blown every morning after Shakharit (morning prayer service) **serving as a call to repentance**. Personally, I see this as the most significant meaning to the picture for all of us alive today. The meaning of the word repent is to turn away from sin. Abstain from any unrighteous act or thought.

The blowing of the trumpet in ancient Israel had two primary functions. The first was to call a solemn assembly: that is, when the children of Israel were to be summoned to God's presence, the trumpet was blown (Ex. 19:13, 17, 19: Num. 10:2). And second, when Israel, under divine direction, was to go to war, the trumpet was to be blown (Num. 10:9; Jud. 7; Jer. 4:19-21). Joshua blew the shofar in the conquest of Jericho (Josh. 6:20). Gideon blew the trumpet in the battle with the Midianites (Jud. 7:18). Nehemiah commanded that the trumpet be blown in the event of attack when rebuilding the walls of Jerusalem (Neh. 4:18).

The prophets of Israel repeatedly revealed a future when God would again directly intervene in the ill-fated plans of mankind. They called that day "the day of the Lord" (Isaiah 13:6-13; Ezek. 13:3-8; 30:2-3; Joel 1:15; 3:14-16; Amos 5:18-20; Zeph. 1:14-2:3; Zech. 14:1-4; Mal. 4:5-6). In connection with his second coming to earth, the Messiah Jesus will call His own to Himself and then go to war against the anti-Christ. It is the blowing of a trumpet which will signal those two events. *2 Thessalonians 4:16-17 "For the Lord himself shall descend from heaven with a shout, with the voice of the archangel, and with the trump of God: and the dead in Christ (Messiah) shall rise first: Then we which are alive and remain shall be caught up together with them in the clouds, meet the Lord in the air; and so shall we ever be with the Lord.*

I Corinthians 15:51-52 ...we shall not all sleep, but we shall all be changed, in a moment, in the twinkling of an eye, at the last trump: for the trumpet shall sound, and the dead shall be raised incorruptible, and we shall be changed, KJV. There is a distinct difference in a shofar and a trumpet. I felt that I must cover the possibilities of this sign significant to the blowing of the shofar and prayer, because the man shown next to him is in fact praying.. Jesus said this about the last days before he would return. Mark 13:34-37 For the son of man (Jesus) is like a man taking a far journey, who left his house, and gave authority to his servants, and to every man his work, and commanded the porter to watch. Watch ye therefore; for ye know not when the master of the house cometh, at evening, or at midnight, or at cockcrow, or in the morning. Lest coming suddenly, he find you sleeping. And what I say to you I say unto all, Watch.

As we continue to examine this one last scene we see the second figure of a person standing beside the shofar blower. The significant posture of this man indicates that he has tilted his head forward, closed his eyes and placed his hands in folded position up to his face. Surely, he is praying at the same time that the trumpet is being sounded. I must say at this particular time of discovery, when this very sign is being discovered and revealed, this should be a serious time of prayer. Clearly, God is leaving one final thought in our discovery. Attention! Pray! We must ask for the forgiveness of our sins. We must pray for the Peace of Jerusalem (Ps. 122:6). We must pray for an abundance of Christian workers and dedicate ourselves to spread the good news of Jesus's Love. We must pray for each of our nations wherever you live in the world. We must pray for the leaders of these nations. When I mentioned praying for the peace of Jerusalem as mentioned in Psalms 122:6 were you thinking about a peaceful settlement agreement to hostilities there? Yes, but that is not exactly the full completeness of the matter although peace among all people living there is definitely desired. You and I must think toward the fulfillment of ultimate Peace. We are to pray for the continued fulfillment of the Kingdom of God, looking forward to the Prince of Peace Jesus to sit on his throne in Jerusalem. As you and I continue to do the work of Christ Jesus expanding the Kingdom (the Kings Domain, His Dominion) then we are acting on this prayer in preparation for that day to come.

Prayer is one of the most important aspects of any Christian's life. It is our communication with Father God. One question you may be asking yourself, "does God hear my prayers?" Well, you must examine yourself first of all and determine your situation with God. Are you a true believer, doing the will of God, serving God? *In Proverbs 15:29 The Lord is far from the wicked (those who do not serve God, Mal.3:18): but he heareth the prayer of the righteous (those who serve God, Mal. 3:18), KJV.* Also see *Proverbs 28:9 He that turneth away his ear from hearing the law (word of God), even his prayer shall be abomination (not worthy of hearing), KJV.* Also see 1 Peter 3:7. If you are in this situation away from God...you do not have to remain there. Become a Christian as we covered in the previous chapter and get to know God personally. If you have drifted away he will take you back with gentle love.

The word of God is absolutely filled with his love for hearing the prayers of those that love him. In *Lamentations 3:24-25 The Lord is my portion, saith my soul; therefore will I hope in him. The Lord is good unto them that wait for him, to the soul that seeketh him, KJV. 1 Peter 3:12 For the eyes of the Lord are over the righteous, and his ears are open to their prayers: but the face of the Lord is against them that do evil. Hebrews 11:6 But without faith it is impossible to please God; for he that cometh must believe that he is, and that he is a reward of them that diligently seek him, KJV.* Isn't it interesting that these last five words 'them that diligently seek him' are there? God wants serious, deliberate devotion. We cannot give up seeking spiritual fulfillment, having anxiousness or even the opposite… mild complacency. In *John 14:13 Jesus says And whatever ye shall ask in my name, that will I do, that the Father may be glorified in the son, KJV.*

As Christians we must keep ourselves occupied with living out the love of Christ toward the world around us. We are the Church. *Ephesians 2:19 Now, therefore, ye are no more strangers and sojourners, but fellow citizens with the saints, and of the household of God; and are built upon the foundation of the apostles and prophets, Jesus Christ himself being the chief corner stone, in whom all the building fitly framed together groweth unto an holy temple in the the Lord; in whom ye also are built together for an habitation of God through the Spirit, KJV.* You and I are growing in the knowledge of God through his word. Each one of us fitted together to do the loving work of God, with each of us doing according to how God has equipped us, I Corinthians 12:1-31.

If I do not have Love I am nothing. All people of the world around us desire to have this one most important missing meaningful fact of life. I Corinthians 13:1-13 reveal's much about this. Love is to continue long through difficult times no matter the issue without strife or malice, Love is Kindness to everyone. Love does not envy those things which you do not have.

Love does not bring pride in your own conceit, willingly placing yourself above others in your own accomplishments, desires, and goals to the other persons hurt. Love does not behave itself unseemly, appearing of no good character. Love does not seek its own reward. Love is not being easily provoked to anger. Love is not thinking and plotting to do evil.

Love is not rejoicing in evil iniquity such as personal revenge or any other sin. Love rejoices in truth. Love bears all things replacing discouragement. Love believes all truth of the word of God, building faith resulting in ultimate endurance. Love never fails, it is of Gods perfect design intent and purpose.

The Trumpet

Now we focus our attention on the nearby scene found in 2019. You see a man about to blow a trumpet, it is only inches from his mouth. The fact that the mouth piece is near to his mouth could represent a more nearness of time of its fulfillment. That can be said with surety, we are closer today than yesterday, which can always be said. No man knows the day or hour, when the son of man comes.

This picture holds a definite message for us today and it is one of absolute joy of expectation. God is saying, "I am emphasizing what I have said before, at the last trumpet sound, I am announcing the arrival of my son, the Lion of the tribe of Judah (Jesus) to rule and reign over all the earth." Notice the male lion's head appears near the end of the trumpet? That is our clue. See the hands of the people are upraised as if welcoming someone! Nothing more can be said. This is exactly what is shown here, nothing more nothing less. A picture of absolute encouragement, and joy of expectation.

Revelation 11:15 Then the seventh angel sounded; and there were loud voices in heaven, saying,"The kingdom of the world hsa become the kingdom of our Lord and of His Christ; and He will reign forever and ever."

What we have all been looking foreward to will then be fulfilled. Jesus comes back to rule and reign from Jerusalem over all the earth. He will put all things in order, no more wars in the world, peace will exist everywhere bythe prince of peace Jesus.

Message in Pictures with the Word of God

Now, after reading all of the scripture information about each picture we can put them all together in message form. The first reference was to "look down from above and see that it is Jesus our High Priest and King of Kings by evidence of the wounds that he suffered on the cross to redeem man-kind. *I Father God, created a covenant with Abraham, to establish the blood line for my son Jesus to be born into the world. God's children must appear before the judgment seat of Christ Jesus to receive according to your life that you have lived, so be careful how you live your life. My son Jesus is real. Here are his baby pictures! Here also are pictures of his crucifixion. Set before you is life or death. You are my sheep that I love dearly. I want you to cross over into a life of protection by shepherds of whom I have chosen that must follow my Son's example of the Good Shepherd. Lastly…Attention! Pray!*

Closing thoughts

Most importantly of all, Jesus is shown prominently in this land. Other countries and continents do not show any, there are no non-Christian figures or symbols shown anywhere. I hope you've enjoyed this exciting journey. It has been an exciting opportunity and enlightening revelation each week during my continuing discovery. Revelation is still coming forth and I am writing a second book to cover another important fact filled aspect of this wonderful marvel. A video is now complete and can be seen by going to timeclockrevelation you tube or going to the web site www.timeclockrevelation.com and going to the upper right hand corner and clicking on "The Video."

Prayer

One of the most important things you can do is pray. Talk to Father God often, he loves you very much. After seeing the video, thank him for this wonderful panorama of pictures he has created.

"Lord heavenly Father please bless the readers of this book in health, in wisdom, in spiritual growth and peaceful joy. Lord, as people of faith read this testimonial of what you have done for me, let there be awe inspiring words from you that touch hearts and move them toward a closer relationship with you. Thank you Lord, for building greater faith and hope by your awesome creative work on the surface of the Earth. Please bring secure lasting wholesome, peaceful, loving relationships together among peoples. To calm lives in ways that are restorative to persons in need. Let there be light shown upon your word that fills – in, builds up, increases faith, and anchors your truth. Amen.

With Sincere Love and Thankfulness
Darrell K. Jackson.

Jesus before the Sanhedron.

Jesus praying in the garden of Gethsemine.

THE SIGN OF CHRIST

Jesus heals sick man.

Jesus heals sick men.

Disciples look on as Jesus heals.

Jesus heals sick lady.

THE SIGN OF CHRIST

Jesus heals baby in basket.

Jesus hols baby lambs.

In the days of John the Baptist the world was full of violence.

Lady heals with many people looking on.

THE SIGN OF CHRIST

Roman soldier observes healing.

Jesus looks on as people continue in his teachings.

A blind man is healed.

www.ingramcontent.com/pod-product-compliance
Lightning Source LLC
LaVergne TN
LVHW091557060526
838200LV00036B/882